Medieval Cooking

in Today's Kitchen

GREG JENKINS

Schiffer Publishing Ltd

4880 Lower Valley Road • Atglen, PA 19310

Other Schiffer Books on Related Subjects:
Beer Brewing for Everyone, Michael Hlatky, 978-0-7643-4492-1

Aroma Kitchen: Cooking with Essential Oils, Sabine Hönig and Ursula Kutschera, 978-0-7643-4793-1

Library of Congress Control Number: 2015942225

Designed by John P. Cheek
Cover design by Danielle D. Farmer
Type set in Cloister Balck BT/Sabon LT Std

ISBN: 978-0-7643-4842-6
Printed in China

Published by Schiffer Publishing, Ltd.
4880 Lower Valley Road
Atglen, PA 19310
Tel.: (610) 593-1777; Fax: (610) 593-2002
E-mail: Info@schifferbooks.com

For our complete selection of fine books on this and related subjects, please visit our website at www.schifferbooks.com. You may also write for a free catalog.

This book may be purchased from the publisher. Please try your bookstore first.

We are always looking for people to write books on new and related subjects. If you have an idea for a book, please contact us at proposals@schifferbooks.com.

Schiffer Publishing's titles are available at special discounts for bulk purchases for sales promotions or premiums. Special editions, including personalized covers, corporate imprints, and excerpts can be created in large quantities for special needs. For more information, contact the publisher.

For my mother, Inez Hall

Contents

The Cook, by J. Amman, ca. sixteenth century. *Courtesy of Society for Creative*

edieval Cooking in Today's Kitchen is written to honor the women and men who found their faith through personal integrity and self-reflection at a time when their lives were fraught with threat and intrigue, when they were denied certain freedoms and when fear and poverty made existence almost intolerable. I must also honor the intrepid spirit of those intriguing peoples—the Paganus folk. The term originally referred to the common man and woman of ancient times who learned to create and survive from the rudimentary aspects of their times. Through their tenacious, often ferocious, courage to go on in times of stress and sickness, and through war, famine, and upheaval, they have helped form every culture around the world today. Indeed, the way we understand our modern customs can be directly attributed to our great ancestors, which, more often than not, were the Paganus common folks living on land owned by the pampered nobility.

Today the term Pagan points more toward the spiritual practices of simple peoples. It conjures images of maidens dancing skyclad in honor of Diana, the goddess of the hunt, to draw down prosperity and blessings, thus re-creating the spirit that has been part of the human condition since the day man first stood upright and threw rocks at the moon, having discovered a harmonious way to honor the things they saw and could not see. These were people who felt a natural reverence toward their world.

Mankind has changed very little since those days, as we can see in the modern ritual of every religion. Through song and praise, dress and stature, custom and the presentation of gifts, and even through spirits and foods, we are like our ancestors at every juncture. The negative side, of course, is intolerance toward those of rival faiths or cultures. All of us can relate to the uneasiness and anxiety of the religious zealots consumed with vengeance and hate. In contrast, however, stand the modern-day Paganus folk and the Neopagan concept of the three-fold law, which basically instructs that all that our acts will be followed by the same acts in kind, whether good or evil.

As modern pagans have all but abandoned the concept of a hell with pits of fire and smoldering brimstone, there is a reverence for what many of us take for granted. Nature and the sum of its many gifts, including food and the means for human survival, are considered sacred gifts for which we should be grateful. Indeed, it is a common juncture of such a spirit that allows us to celebrate in a time-honored manner that directly shines of the ancient. The Paganus folk of old—those simple dwellers of the ancient world, whether hailing from north or south, east or west—formed many of the lifestyles we see today. Though each holiday marks a specific occasion, whether to honor a god, a goddess, or a season, it might surprise us just how connected we are as a people. Regardless of faith, we all have one thing in common—devotion to the many aspects of our heritage that make up the whole, including many forms of folk customs such as music and dance, oral traditions, and folklore, and my personal favorite of all—the culinary arts.

Having studied these peoples and their customs, I can honestly say that without the tenacious efforts of those who saved to memory the fine and proper methods of cookery, wine and beer making, and all related entities of gastronomy, we would be a rather bland creature, indeed. Thankfully people did take note of their food and beverage-making in detail, keeping ledgers very much like a chemist keeps his notations on how to make and remake potions. And like the chemist, the cook of old would have passed down his or her collections to acolyte and apprentice so that they, too, could keep that tradition alive for centuries to come.

Like the ancient magi who kept only a few of their original texts of sacred magic on hand, the most studious scholars transcribed more than one text and offered them only to the noblest students who held them in respect, added to them, and perhaps illustrated them, and then passed them down. This process is identical to that of the ancient cook who would have followed the exact method to the letter. Although only a scant number of people would have been able to read, let alone write, the ancient cook would have used basic illustrations to show herbs, vegetables, fruits, cattle, fowl, and fish, perhaps adding symbols to represent amounts and equations that marked them as personal recipes.

By the nineteenth century, these ancient books of cookery had been deciphered, and many of the antiquated symbols and illustrations found a modern recipe that we can understand today. Yet, one cannot help but wonder what it would have been like to have feasted in a great hall of some medieval castle in England, or supped in a modest cottage in Wales or Scotland during the Tudor age. One might wonder just how the Paganus people of old—surfs and laborers, farmers and fisherman—lived and survived, what they ate and drank, and how they celebrated their holidays. It might be surprising just how little has changed.

For many Paganus folk, as for those in the contemporary faiths today, the vibrations of the past are very much alive. Certainly pagans of all lineages, whether those involved in Wicca, Hellenism, or sects of the Germanic and Romano pagan faiths or those within Kemetism and the Semitic cultures, as well as those who follow polytheism, animism, pantheism, and any number of the shamanic faiths, all hold dear their ancient past. Although these people live an average, modern lifestyle during the workweek, they hold within them a reverence for what has for centuries garnished ridicule and violence, not unlike that of the inquisitions centuries ago. Their independent spirit and gentle demeanor moves forward into the twenty-first century with equal reverence and resolve. They bring the past—the song and dance, ritual and prayer, and festivals and feasts—to our humble tables.

The great wheel of the year—praising and honoring the earth, her seasons and her gifts

In giving thanks for the foods and customs we now enjoy and take for granted, we sometimes ask ourselves how the Paganus folk showed their gratitude in the ancient world. Most Americans think of the pilgrims and their thanksgiving feast, which fostered a belief that all was well for the ancient settlers. Nothing could be farther from the truth, however, as the first colonists almost blinked out of existence and their interaction with the natives was disastrous. Yes, they survived and went on to make history, keeping many time-honored traditions from fading into obscurity.

Many of us hold dear the history of family ancestors who predate the Americans by centuries and are as diverse as the many faiths that identify them. I certainly regard my Welsh-Gaelic background as the primary source of my being. And I happily show my gratitude to my rich ancestry in the way I celebrate and give honor, and shall do so all my days. This simple edict should be shared with all peoples and of all faiths, as doing so brightens the world. This is the very reason our ancestors survived; more than waging wars, upholding dogmatic religions, or dominating others, it is the festive aspects of our traditions that continue on long after we're gone.

As we prepare for the approaching holidays, whatever they may be for you, we should know a little about these festive events in order to make the best of our efforts. Though the majority of Paganus folks honored variations of many backgrounds and traditions, the most commonly observed practices are likely based in Greek, Roman, Germanic, and Anglo-Celtic traditions passed down in oral traditions. Take, for example the legend of the Oak King and the Holly King in Welsh-Celtic folklore. These two seasonal gods battle each year for domination of the land and sky. Each wins at various dates and times, one usurping the other for a period of time. The Holly King obviously denotes the hearty, steadfast leaves of the holly bush, which strives through the winter season, just as the mighty Oak King represents the healthy season of spring and the autumn solstice. Each has a place and purpose, and each has a separate manner in which to be remembered. Though history will always be remembered differently as the ages pass, it's important to be faithful to your own method with as much zeal and happiness as you can muster—for your loved ones, your family, and your creed.

It might amaze us to find that most of our holiday traditions are founded in pagan traditions. Behold the hearty Holly King of ancient Celtic folklore. He was viewed as a large man with a great beard and was often seen wearing a brilliant green or red suit common of the day, trimmed with white fur. He was always seen sporting fresh holly leaves in his hair and beard and had a knack for avoiding human capture. For modern -day pagans he might symbolize the Green Man, a creature that has as many guises as there are leaves on the trees of the world, though for contemporary Christians, he bears a keen resemblance to Saint Nicholas of Catholic and Orthodox origins—the patron saint of sailors, archers, thieves, and yes, children, too. Few people realize that Santa Claus, that jolly fat man who descends from the heavens to bestow gifts on children everywhere, is actually a fourth-century rendition of the great Holly King of Celtic folklore. There are many other similarities between modern belief systems and the traditional holidays observed by Paganus folk all over the world.

The power of history to transcend time is likely the most potent aspect of the human condition. We might ask ourselves the reason for celebrating the holidays as we do, perhaps assuming that modern religions started the faith-related customs we observe today. However, the primarily Christian-themed holidays like Easter and Christmas are actually of pagan origin. For example, the evergreen tree was used in pre-Christian Germanic winter rites representing the legend of the donar oak, which may also be akin to the legend of Thor's Oak in Norse mythology or that of Yggdrasil, a tree of life motif that held great honor among the ancient Vikings and Germanic peoples. In fact, we can see this concept all over the world, so it was not a Christian invention, but merely a way to cover up the ancient pagan Yule Winter Solstice tradition that fell near the same date. In truth, the Yule solstice that takes place on December 25 represented the birth of the sun for many pre-Christian peoples, as in the birth of Mithra for Roman pagans. Such occasions were often celebrated with pine or oak logs burning on great pyres, the faithful walking in processions with lit candles and decorating the evergreen trees in their forests. In short, the later mannerisms were simply a church-devised mandate to wash away the heathen faiths and genteelly convert the masses to the new religion.

Easter has similar parallels. For Christians, the crucifixion and resurrection of Christ signifies living, and then death, and then back to life in an altered state of perfection, basically representing a supernatural example of nature in progress. The ancient Paganus folk would have recognized this process as part of a great wheel, where one season begets the next, and so on, until it starts over again. For the pagan Spring Equinox, or Ôstara, we don't see the customary chocolate bunnies and sugary marshmallow chicks, though the meaning is similar in many respects. For Christians, Easter honors Christ and his ascension to heavenly perfection, where for pagans, Ôstara honors the rebirth of spring, the growth of fruit and grains, and the spawning of new life. Therefore, there never really is a death, per se, merely a pattern of transition to expect and appreciate in our own customary ways.

The season of Beltane, along with Imbolc and Ôstara, represents the final spring equinox festivals of fertility, honoring both human and animal propagation, as well as nature in all its guises. For Celtic and many European Paganus folk, Beltane serves as the second primary gateway festival, with Samhain rounding out the wheel. In many ways, Beltane is a festive celebration that honors the spring and midsummer equinoxes, fulfilling the summer solstice, signifying the light and strength of this time of year. It traditionally signifies the arrival of summer and a time to give thanks for our blessings and celebrate growth in all its glory.

For many pagans today, Beltane appears like a grand spectacle, where children and maidens are dressed in colorful garb, often with flowing robes and bright shirts. Men and woman dance around the maypole tethered to bright colored ropes, and young men attach garlands and herbal hawthorn boughs above the doors of the ladies they desire, while woman will jump over fire pits to beseech a favorable birthing or to become with child. Some will skip and dance around these fires for a prosperous year ahead, while others watch for faerie folk to cause playful mischief, as the realms between ours and theirs is thin. Indeed, as Beltane serves as a polar opposite to the darker season of the autumn solstice and the arrival of Samhain, it is a time of great joy and heartfelt gaiety.

The celebration of Lithia follows and represents the summer solstice. Although a relatively recent invention by occult scholar Aidan A. Kelly in 1973, it is nonetheless based on an important time observed by the ancients as a way to honor the sun, which, of course, helped grow the crops and fruit trees, in turn sustaining life for the community. It continues to be a time to renew past promises, a time when lord and lady would handfast in grand ceremonies with music, food, and joy. It was a time to set barriers against evil and its influences on the people, when the ancients would cast great fires across the countryside to frighten off demons and other naysayer devils from encroaching on the village. It was a way to gather people together and praise the light of the day and the height of summer, as soon the dark season would come. When it did, the chance for famine and sickness was always greater. The right amount of honor and worship would better the community's chance to survive and prosper during the harsh winter months.

As the great seasonal wheel continues to rotate, we find ourselves at the juncture of the three main autumn festivals of Lammas, also known as Lughnasa, named after the Celtic god Lugh. The festival of Lammas is a time for prayer and praise for the harvest; the very name signifies the term for "loaf-mass." Many Paganus folk would have poured milk and honey into the earth for a good crop and baked breads with little effigies of the Celtic god carved into them to honor the god and the season, which gives life to the agrarian and hunter alike. It is a time of reflection too, where without a gainful harvest the people of old might have starved during the winter months.

The autumn equinox follows with *Gwyl canol Hydref*, what is known today as Mabon, named for the Welsh god of divine youth and love. Mabon, or the Harvest Tide for many pagans today, is also a term coined by occult scholar Aidan A. Kelly. It represents a seasonal holiday for thanksgiving and sharing; but also for saying goodbye for a time. Like the blessings from well-wishers before going on a great journey, the ancients would have prepared group ceremonies to offer respect for the time and season they were currently in, and plead to the goddesses and gods for a pleasant and mild winter. In short, the ancients believed that the sun god would return to embrace the goddess when the great wheel rotates back and the stars are right again.

The Mabon season is a time to gather boughs of wheat to place around the altars, and for drinking spiced wines and brews in praise of the bountiful harvest, to dance around the fire and sing songs of happiness and tribute, as doing so is said to drive away the sadness and melancholy that often accompanies the dark winter months. The Mabon holiday is also a time to make new vows, whether to rededicate a marriage, propose engagements before the community, or promise change in one's life.

As the autumn season wanes to winter, we observe the pagan New Year, Samhain, likely the most observed holiday in all cultures in one way or another. Also known as *Oidhche Shamhna* or Third Harvest, Samhain is not unlike *Dia de los Muertos*, the Day of the Dead celebration observed by the Mexicans today. Both traditionally pay respects to departed family and loved ones once a year by feasting, singing, and dancing in their honor. It is a time to spend with the departed and talk of family and current affairs, though here the similarities end. For the Celts and modern-day Paganus folk, Samhain represents the community's third and final harvest and is regarded as one of the four Greater Sabbats, creating a high holiday for celebration, honor, and reflection.

The modern concept of Halloween, with its childish aspects such as masked, candy-craving children and their silly tricks come to mind, but make no mistake; this was likely the most important season for the ancients. With the world positioned just right for the souls of the dead to return, the ancients would have the chance to make amends to lost friends and family, and make a resolution to those they wronged in life. It was also a time when the spirits of the dead and other creatures from the netherworld could arrive to wreak havoc, so sacrifices would often take place, where apples, corn, chickens, and other animals were offered to the gods and goddesses for a favorable year ahead. To this end, celebrations would be great events, with bonfires set around the countryside to light the night sky and act as a sacrament. For modern pagans, now is a time for blessings and prayers; a celebration of hope marks the coming of the new season as we return to the Yule season and the Winter Solstice, where the great wheel arrives at its apex once more.

The art of the ritual for all occasions: methods for soulful expressions of faith and joy

Now that we have a brief outline of the many holidays and festivals that have and continue to inspire Paganus folk all over the world, let's look at some ways we can express our devotion through the use of colors and settings, as well as foods and libations, to capture the feeling of the ancient past in all its glory. Certainly, as the majority of Paganus folk today are able to connect themselves directly to the issues, customs, and even clothing styles of our ancient ancestors, it should be safe to assume that when we stage a gathering or grand feast, we shall do the same. And, as we are prone to connecting to all things esoteric and what might be considered by some as completely fantastic, we have a gift for channeling the thought and spirit of our ancestors with great zeal.

In late December 2010, while visiting historic Stonehenge in Wiltshire, England, I had the wonderful opportunity to take part in the annual Festival of Yule marking the ancient New Year and the start of longer days and shorter nights. The event was massive, beginning just before the sun had risen for the day. It was chilly, with a slight blanket of snow on the ground, but there was a pleasant warmth radiating from the more than 2,000 people who mingled about. As the sun began its accent, the sky became like a pink and gold fire, with shimmering purple clouds. Then the chants began in rhythmic fashion, along with music from instruments I had never seen before, such as concertinas and dulcimers, penny whistles and wooden flutes, mandolins and fiddles, and baroque musettes and bodhrán drums, creating a feeling of the old, yet also of a family gathering. It was astonishing and beautiful, and an event I won't soon forget.

The crowd was still as a Druid priest, dressed in white robes and clad in animal-skin boots with a red stole draped around his neck, held his staff high above his head and spoke the words, "Peace in the west, and peace in the east," with a soulful ardor. As he continued, the people responded in kind, just they would in any congregation. This is but one example of how all races and creeds show respect to their gods and goddesses, transcending their present day concerns, and dropping back to a time before we led such fast and furious lifestyles. In spite of the hurried world we live in, we can travel back to a time when the festivals were great and the gatherings truly meaningful.

As we begin, let us consider the great wheel of the year, the seasonal calendar of events used by our ancient ancestors. Using its holiday observances as a baseline for how we'll honor the seasons and our friends, we'll begin with the simplest method to ensure each season is represented properly. Whether setting up a festival or arranging a feast for friends and family, consider decorating with the colors natural elements that best respond to that season. For the Yule Solstice, one might choose to follow the old traditions and use colors like reds, greens, blues, and whites. One might incorporate these colors either in table cloths, banners, or clothing, and have plenty of mistletoe, holly, and evergreen bundled into wreaths to adorn the walls, tables, and doorways. As I have several massive oak trees on my land, I have an ample supply of the magical parasite-herb mistletoe. It holds the mysterious scents and colors of ancient winter celebrations. Such practices bring peace, but also ground a location as a sacred place. One might also add many candles to brighten the event.

One tradition I honor is the Yule Eve candle, which is a good two feet in length and about ten inches wide. The candle is a dark mulberry red, which I consecrate with the essential oils and gentle aroma of pine and mistletoe. I also smolder the resin incense of myrrh and frankincense during this season; it is said to create a psychic bond with nature and one's home. Such candles and resins can be purchased or made in the traditional colors used by the ancients. The Celts, Britons, Germanic, and Scandinavian peoples favored forest greens to denote nature, dark reds for the many berries and apples, and snow whites and dark blues to signify the stars, snow, and the night sky. If you wish, you can wrap the cut mistletoe or evergreen pine around the base of the candle to add to the flare of the light and scent, but be cautions with the mistletoe if you have children or animals, as the berries are poisonous. Simply pluck off the berries and return them to nature.

As food and drink go, it's always good to start with a warming drink such as Metheglin, which is a flavorful ginger wine. I always have a homemade Yuletide Wassail and tasty Hippocras made from genuine recipes to serve my guests. These are authentic libations that can be traced back to the English Isles and to the time of King Arthur. Indeed, no celebration is complete without such a start to the new season ahead. For breads and hors d'oeuvres I like to offer simple and time-honored dishes like squash muffins and funge pasties, delicious spicy mushroom pasties, and full-bodied pottages like pease pottage, a hearty split pea soup; stewed pompion, a spicy pumpkin soup; and cawl cymreig or cawl, a thick, hearty Welsh stew. The main meal might consist of coffyn pyes, which are little spicy meat pies; roasted honey chicken; Cornish sausages and fried rissoles; and spicy mincemeat tarts. In addition, the tables would be adorned with platters of seasonal fruits and assorted nuts, and I might serve side dishes that would have been staples for our ancestors, such as frumenty, a medieval-era wheat stuffing; clapshot potatoes; and a wide selection of vegetable and soufflé dishes for my vegan friends.

Finally, as the meal begins to wane, we take a time out to give praise for our happiness and blessed occasions and cast away our doubts and trivial concerns. We give thanks to that which we believe and honor those who are in need. This part of the evening is a ceremony and can be more serious, but only for the moment. Soon music and song commences and dancing erupts. When we tire a bit, we'll sit near my fire pit and reminisce with a glass of wine or coffee. Eventually I'll serve one of my favorite ending dishes, such as medieval-style apple and pear fritters dusted with powdered sugar. I usually have authentic figgie hobbin, which is thick pudding served with clotted cream, as well as spicy ginger bread, fruit confit, and assorted sweets. All in all, I have never had a complaint, only happy and soul-rested friends ready to take on the coming year.

As other holidays come and go, you'll find that each requires a unique representation, and the individual expression applied to it will make all the difference. Whatever your path, faith, or background, the more reverence you show for your heritage, the better the chance that the sentiment will be passed on for years to come. Embrace the lesser- known aspects of your heritage by showcasing the details, whether in the music or dress, foods or libations; express your singular differences with flair and purpose. Let your feast be an echo of your ancestor's humble past with fervent faith and soulful compassion. Let your spirit soar!

Feast scene from Richard Pynson's 1526 edition of *The Canterbury Tales. Courtesy of Society for Creative Anachronism*

Our feasting heritage: historic recipes fit for lord and lady, magi and nave

"Sing a song of sixpence a pocket full of rye, four and twenty blackbirds baked in a pye. When the pye was opened the birds began to sing, oh wasn't that a dainty dish to set before the king…?"

—*Sing a song of sixpence by George Stevens, ca. 1744*

This quaint children's rhyme expresses a practice believed to have been committed by King Henry VIII as a gesture to adversaries, allies, and potential allies, meaning that there was something "hidden" in the gift for the receiver, such as an estate or land. Yet history suggests that such cooking practices did indeed occur, as in Shakespeare's *Twelfth Night* (1602), where a large pie made of rye flower was partially baked and then filled from the side with living children, presumably "naughty boys." Despite the great bard's humorous adaptations, fully cooked pies made with blackbirds, or more appropriately pigeons, were served as a meal in some homes. Unappetizing as they sound, consider also braised hedgehog made with honey and garlic sauce, or extremely rare rabbit served in its own blood as a sauce, or perhaps boiled dog. These were common meals for the poor and wealthy alike.

Stranger things have been brought to our attention. On April 1, 2012, the British Library reported that a rare cookbook was discovered in its archives, reputed to be that of Geoffrey Fule, master chef in the court of Philippa of Hainault, Queen of England, ca. 1328 to 1369. The recipes contained the aforementioned dishes for blackbird pye and braised hedgehog, and another that astounded researchers and staff—for roasted unicorn! Without a doubt, the recipe is raising more questions than answers, with some asking: Did such creatures actually exist, or was this just a tongue-in-cheek joke among cooks of the day? The report was accompanied with excellent, full-color illustrations of cooking staff preparing a unicorn, some stoking a fire beneath the mythical creature, a woman carrying a basket containing its head, and more. Yes, this report came out on April Fools' Day. But such recipes may not be far off from truth. The ancients did, in fact, eat some foods we would never consume today.

Regardless, there are many ancient recipes that will work nicely for any event or get-together. With help from several universities, the British Library, the National Library of France, and family and colleagues, I was able to unearth some of the best and most beloved foods in all of history.

While researching rare but palatable dishes from the medieval and High Renaissance periods, I found recipes that would astound, and quite frankly, sicken most people today. The recipes for boiled dog and braised hedgehog brought to mind the dark ages and starvation, while recipes for grilled and stuffed porpoise made me glad I lived in modern times. Yet, as I looked further, I found foods and libations that would have been a sheer delight, reminding me of the many Renaissance fairs and church and university functions I've attended over the years. I found a connection with the ancient and modern Paganus folk alike.

Because the reality of cooking in medieval and Renaissance times could have been as hazardous to your health as any battle or plague, some of the recipes herein have been slightly altered from their original usage. Indeed, between over-salting foods, which was once done to preserve meats and fish, and the consumption of potentially deadly plants and animals, the reasoning for these updates become clear. Regardless, with many of these dishes, it may be necessary to replace some ingredients from the original recipes. For instance, you may substitute Cornish hens for pigeons, and large chickens for capons, or otherwise castrated roosters. Moreover, you should also use fresh meat rather than over-salted, over-aged, or unrefrigerated meats. Fish dishes, however, remain virtually the same today, minus the use of some spices, which may have been too sweet and exotic for today's culinary aficionado.

Beverages from Renaissance and colonial times were also greatly festive, and quite potent, and so, as with any other alcoholic beverages, the drinks here should be consumed with care. In re-creating many of the libations noted in this book, most were actually quite simple and enjoyable to make. Others were more difficult and time consuming to prepare, but all were certainly worth the effort. Obtaining the herbs and spices should be simple enough, as most grocers and health food stores will carry them. In addition, many wholesale merchants and specialty grocers will sell even the most difficult-to-find spices and herbs at your request.

The one thing to remember above all when creating your dining occasion is that it should never be plain, boring, or without levity. Instead, your feast should be plentiful, and your banquet a celebration of life! As the gift of our ancient ancestors was one of cheerful thanks for the bounty of their sumptuous repast, and the pride of their kingdom, village, and home, so too should your feast resound the same thanksgiving. So, whatever the event, whether it be at your group's meetings, for a high holiday or solstice, or when entertaining for family and friends, treat yourself and your honored guests to an occasion they will not soon forget.

Woodcut from Hans Burgkmair, early sixteenth century. *Courtesy of Society for Creative Anachronism, Arts and Sciences of the Middle Ages and Renaissance*

Foods and Cooking in the Ancient World

When we think of eating a meal today, we might think of opening a can of ravioli, tossing something into the microwave, or stopping by a local diner or fast food restaurant for a quick meal. Despite our modern-day conveniences, dining is often hum-drum. In Renaissance times, however, the dining experience could rival our modern-day festivals. Despite the daily battle to survive, with constant threat of invasion from neighboring armies or the menace of a plague that could wipe out an entire countryside, life was still enjoyable, especially when it came to food and drink.

Despite being steadfast field laborers, the ancient Paganus people would take meals three or four times a day from late morning to late night. Breakfast was a loaf of dark or wheat-grain bread, and, if they were lucky, a shard of hard cheese. The noon-day meal might be a bowl of broth or stew, more bread, and perhaps a tankard of ale. As night approached and the workday wrapped up, there might be another meal consisting of the same hard bread and cheese, and perhaps a shank of mutton or bowls of soup or stew, depending on the family's wealth. On special occasions, commoners might be invited to a banquet or village feast, which would likely be the highlight of their year.

This meal would be hearty and might go down in history. A noble's evening meal, for instance, might consist of two or three large courses including a variety of meats such as beef, pork, mutton, poultry, venison, and fish, all gracing the tables like a work of art. Breads, pastries, cheeses, fruits, and nuts were plentiful, and every gathering had plenty of spiced wines and ales to liven the evening. The noble's feast would be quite the spectacle, designed to show off generosity and wealth.

These banquets sometimes serviced 500 or more guests and literally required more food than would feed an average army. History tells us that some of these legendary feasts required as many as fifty oxen and cows, 200 geese, and 100 or more pigs, sheep, venison, and lamb to supply the main tables. But that's not all. There would also be hundreds of capons, pigeons, pheasant, and other varieties of fowl, and thousands of fish. To wash it down, there would be barrel upon barrel of ales, wines, and cordials of every flavor, which would flow until the supply expired. The desserts were no less spectacular, consisting of baked tarts, meal wafers, custards, sweet compotes, spiced candies, sugared fruit compotes, exotic jellies, and edible flowers. Sometimes the variety of sweets would out-match the number of main dishes. Such a feast might last all night and into the next day.

Although Paganus folk of the sixteenth to eighteenth centuries had it considerably better than their medieval counterpart, there was still a great division between rich and poor. Broths, stews, cheeses, and curds were the foods of commoners. A staple of the diet was dark bread such as rye or barley, sometimes mixed with bean flour to stretch it. Nobility, however, could afford white breads; it was practically illegal for a commoner to partake in the joys of the white loaf unless a noble was feeling particularly generous that day.

The middle class and minor nobility could afford beef, fowl, fish, and a better variety of grain and breads. They would also have had a better selection of cheeses, fresh and dried fruits, and ales. If they were fortunate, they might have imported spiced wines, and even chocolates from Spain. Each course consisted of several finely prepared dishes, all placed on the table together as a buffet-style family meal. For starters, there would be a thick broth with salt pork; miniature meat pastries would be filled with fish livers or beef marrow. A roasted or boiled meat and saltwater or freshwater fish might be available too, as well as a puree of fish and spices or thick stew.

The second course might have other meat dishes, like tile, which are pieces of chicken or veal, sautéed and slow cooked all day, and served in a thick and spicy-sweet almond sauce over freshly baked bread, and sometimes garnished with more fish or exotic spices, followed by meat pasties and herb-roasted capons. The third course might consist of other fish varieties and a hearty slab of braised venison or beef. Often there would be a thick stuffing called frumenty, which was a common wheat stuffing sautéed in a spicy sauce, as well as roasted bream and fried sweet and spicy mushrooms known as funges.

Dessert would feature a wide array of tarts, and other jellies and pastries shaped like crowns, castles, lions, or other icons of royalty, as well as heavily spiced mulled wines. Imported Seville and Valencia oranges and native fruits and spices were offered to aid in the digestion of the rich foods. In some homes, it was common to eat a small lemon or herb salad at the end of the meal, along with a glass of burgundy or port.

Spices were used in practically every dish. The most common were dried and powdered ginger, anise, nutmeg, cinnamon, clove, mace, saffron, and coarsely ground pepper. Fresh herbs such as parsley, garlic, basil, galingale, rosemary, and thyme were commonplace additions to red meats, fowl, fish, and stews. A special mixture of ground spices was even kept on the table for perking up any bland morsel.

The common spice box, for instance, used in medieval and Renaissance times might consist of ground clove, mace, cardamom, pepper, cinnamon, ginger, and bread crumbs. The cook would keep a spice box in the kitchen, too, used for rubbing spice into not-so fresh meats, along with salts and strong vinegars to keep them edible for months at a time. A similar mixture of ground clove, cinnamon, ginger, and grains of paradise, known as powder fine, added a unique flavor to meats and fish. Indeed, such powder rubs were far spicier and sweeter than foods of our day, and the modern guest will find it strangely delightful. Although many of these recipes are difficult to pronounce and seem difficult to create, this cookbook offers a chance to not only re-create the fascinating meals of yesteryear, but also to experience what dining was like centuries ago.

During my research I discovered a cornucopia of authentic recipes that are still in use today. While in Cardiff, Wales some years ago, a long-time friend shared a recipe for caws pobi, otherwise known as Welsh rarebit, which has graced Welsh and English homes for centuries. The recipe was from her great-grandmother's cookbook dated around 1801, though the original recipe likely dates back to the late medieval or early Renaissance era.

In its original tongue, the recipe reads as follows:

Yn gyntaf dylid todi'r menyd mewn sosban cyn ychwanegu'r blawd a'i gogino am ddau funud. I'r gymysgedd yma dylid ychwanegu'r mwstadd, y saws Worcesterchire a'r cwrw. Wedi cogino'r cymysgfa am tua pedwar munud dylid ychwanegu'r caws wedi ei garfellu ychydig wrth ychydig gan sicrhau and yw'n llosgi ar waelod y sosban. Tra mae'r caws yn toddi dylid tostio bara ar un ochor a phan mae'r caws yn barod dylid ei dolldi ar ben ochr amrwd y bar cyn ei roi o dan y gradell i liwio pen y caws (c. 1801).

Without a good interpreter, such a famous dish might have been lost. Fortunately, however, this dish is as popular with the Welsh as a hamburger is to Americans, so it will likely always be with us in one form or another. I came away with an understanding of just how important these traditional meals were to the people who had been saving them since their inception. Prepare to depart the ordinary and lavish your family and friends with the elegance of an ancient era, when galleons and tall ships glided through blue-green waters, when castles and their peopled villages were alive and glowing with life, when Paganus peoples danced in praise to lively music in praise. Prepare to enjoy a robust and vibrant dining experience from a far simpler time.

Chapter 1. Traditional Libations and Spirited Concoctions

OF WINE AND BREW AND SONG, YOUR LIFE BE STRONG AND LONG.

"A meal without wine is like a day without sunshine."
—*Jean-Anthelme Brillat-Savarin (1755-1826)*

The Brewer, by J. Amman, ca. sixteenth century. *Courtesy of Society for Creative Anachronism, Arts and Sciences of the Middle Ages and Renaissance*

Festive cocktails and libations have always held a place of reverence in all classes of society. Whether it was fruit punches and slings, temperate cobblers, hot toddies, sweet bounces, or heavy ales and flips, our ancient cousins had their own unique method for driving away cold and boredom. These ancient peoples would eventually migrate from the English isles and across Europe and then over the seas to the new colonies, bringing with them their festive libations and ways of celebrating. With the Spanish introducing fruity sangrias and dark rums to Cuba and other island seaports, and the port-wine sack, brandy, rye and dark bitters from the English colonizers, such culinary contributions may be the single reason for the festive parties, cocktail hours, and assorted happy occasions we experience today.

In ancient times, noble and Paganus folk alike would have enjoyed alcoholic beverages such as wines, meads, and brews. When they had just the right crop of grapes and berries, they would often experiment, creating rich and tasty cordials made with infusions of fruits, herbs, spices, and sometimes plant extracts. By the time Europeans were relocating to the Americas, they had a much better chance to experiment with the newly discovered rums and white liquors, culminating in many fascinating recipes that exist to this day. Names like Rattle-Skull, Bogus, Stonewall, Blackstrap, and Whistle Belly suggest the many joyous occasions that resulted from our ancestors' curiosity. The following collection of syllabubs, bounces, flips, and cock ales are inspired by direct recipes and culinary folk legends and will delight you and your guests, though there are a variety of libations that go well with these dishes.

When hosting a dinner in the tradition of an ancient feast or banquet, it is important to have the right wine, beer, or ale to create the most enjoyable atmosphere for your guests. I offer these recipes to better detail the various drinks that best suit the meals that follow. Most of the wines and beers listed here may be purchased in fine liquor stores and wineries worldwide. Aperitifs of smoked fish and most dishes containing fowl go well with a white Sancerre or a dry Champaign. A Sauvignon Blanc or dry sherry will go well with hors d'oeuvres, dry canapés, cold meat dishes, veal, and bold soups. Zinfandels, bold Merlots, and deep red table wines complement red meats and pastas, just as Cabernet Sauvignons are good with stout cuts of beef, stews, and roast meats.

Other dishes, like saucy beef and dry or pungent bird entrées, such as pheasant and squab, pair well with mountain red wines, cock ale, and dark and amber beers. Heavy tomato dishes and strong game stews go well with amber ales or red and white Chiantis, and a hearty red Valpolicella complements light fish, veal, and nontraditional pasta dishes. For hams and shellfish dishes consider a white rose, and for egg dishes, a cool white Traminer to bring out the best flavors. Boiled chicken and veal dishes work well with Puligny Montrachet, and you can serve a white Pouilly-Fume with crab, shrimp, and fried fish. Try a red Fleurie or Chambertin with dry meats for the best match.

When serving fruit compotes, sweet cheeses, and roasted nuts, a sweet Stepony raisin wine goes exceedingly well, as does a tart ginger wine or white Sauterne for dry deserts like cakes and sweet breads. So, whether planning for a simple gathering or a solstice or high holiday, here is a healthy selection of festive libations to choose from. Enjoy them in honor of your ancestors and in praise of your honored friends and family!

Hogmanay Berry Bounce
ENGLISH RECIPE, CA. SEVENTEENTH CENTURY

This delightfully fruity drink was an all-time favorite during the Cavalier days, especially with the ladies of the court. Made with cherries, raspberries, or blueberries, this traditional "bounce" recipe will soon become a favorite for any party or feast you will host. Thought to have traveled down from the Scottish highlands, this mixture is believed to have existed during the first mention of whiskey, as expressed in the *Exchequer Rolls of Scotland* in 1495. The word Hogmanay refers to a New Year's event in Scotland, but is actually related to the ancient festivals of the Celts, Vikings, and Anglo-Saxons, where it had various meanings. It represents the festival before Yule but also stands for *hoog min dag*, which means "great love day" to the Flemish; *oge maiden*, meaning "a new morning" to the Celts; *homme est né*, meaning "man is born" to the ancient French, and representing the last day of the year. Today, Hogmanay is marked with the festive torch and bonfire ceremonies observed in Scotland, though this event dates to medieval times. Although there are several variations of this recipe, this one seems to be a historic favorite.

Hogmanay Berry Bounce

Ingredients
1 pound cherries (sour cherries are best)
1 liter Scotch whisky (single malt Scotch is best)
1 cup natural or white sugar

Much like a traditional shrub recipe, first place the berries (raspberries and blackberries work nicely, too) in a medium-sized to large earthen crock or wood cask and add the whisky and sugar. Mash the entire concoction with a potato masher into a fine mush. Strain the mixture through a cheesecloth into another pot, and clean the earthen crock or wood cask of any pulp or seed, making sure to clean with water only, as detergents will leave a residue. Now return the liquid to it, sealing it with a lid or wax paper, wrapped tightly with string. Store in a dark, cool place for at least three weeks for proper fermentation, and then strain once again through cheesecloth into a separate, clean bottle. A glass demijohn or carboy will give it an authentic look. Keep in a cool place and serve in frosted wine or whisky glasses straight up or over ice. Serving sizes vary.

Seafarer's Flip

ENGLISH RECIPE, CA. SEVENTEENTH CENTURY

Traditional flips are strong drinks favored by society's tougher elements, such as the sailors and soldiers who served them so many years ago. It was also a drink that kept the common folk warm during the winter months and was used as a medicinal; they thought it could help with colds and chills. Though any good flip might suit a rugby or football player, when sipped during a cold night, this unique drink will satisfy even the gentlest demeanor.

Seafarer's Flip

Ingredients (per drink)
3 large eggs
3 teaspoons sugar
½ to 1 shot rum
½ shot brandy
12–16 ounces ale or amber beer
dash of cinnamon or nutmeg (optional)

In ancient times, this drink would be made one at a time for each customer. The innkeeper or his barmaid would prepare this drink over the fireplace, placing a red hot "flip iron," or poker into a tall clay tankard or metal flagon. Today, however, the easiest method is done on the stove. I like to prepare the above ingredients for four to six people, depending on the size of my party. Because everyone may not enjoy this drink, you may wish to make one portion to begin with. Place the eggs, sugar, rum, and brandy in a medium saucepan and heat on medium-low for five minutes. Beat with a whisk until frothy, and then simmer on low. (Remember, the above amounts are meant for one large mug, so if you have two people or more, the ingredients double by one.)

When the mixture is nice and warm, place each person's mug, preferably a metal mug or tankard, in front of them and ladle an equal amount in each. Pour in the ale or beer and stir quickly with a spoon. If you have a fireplace and wish to add a little flair to your party, heat a clean iron poker until red, carefully place it in each mug, and briefly stir. This will make it warm, which is always delightful during the winter season.

Hippocras or Tripple

ENGLISH RECIPE, CA. SEVENTEENTH CENTURY

When I make traditional hippocras, flips, or cock ales, I can't help thinking I'm taking a few steps back in time to the age of Queen Elizabeth, when pirates and privateers were cruising the waters or stopping by a pub to have a frothy pint and listen to the tales of Sir Francis Drake. Originally used medicinally, they have been a British Isles standard for centuries and continue to be popular today. These recipes are incredibly easy to make and taste wonderful served chilled in the summer and warm during the winter. Try using different wines to offer a wider selection to your guests.

Hippocras

Ingredients
4 sticks cinnamon
2 ounces powdered cinnamon
½ ounce nutmeg
1 ounce galingale
1 ounce white string ginger
1 ounce grains of paradise
5 whole cloves
1 quart white, rose or red wine
2 cup raw sugar

Combine the spices in a mortar and grind them to a medium-fine to fine powder. The cinnamon, ginger, nutmeg, grain of paradise, and galingale should already be ground, but when adding the whole cloves with the other spices to the mortar, bruising these spices will make them more potent.

Place the powdered spices in an 8-by-8-inch square of cheesecloth and tie with cooking string. Combine the sugar and wine and stir vigorously until the sugar is dissolved. Place the spice sachet in the bottle with the string hanging on the outside, then cork tightly. Store the bottle under your kitchen sink or in a dark closet for at least a week before serving. Then strain the wine and spice mixture through a piece of clean cheesecloth. Pour into a clean bottle and chill overnight. Serve in tankards or large, chilled glasses with sliced fruit and cinnamon sticks. Serves 4 to 6.

Cock Ale or Sack
ENGLISH RECIPE, CA. SIXTEENTH CENTURY

A favorite of soldiers and the common man since ancient times, cock ale likely had the same effect as today's cold beer. During the seventeenth century, Paganus folk drank cock ale year-round, often using it as an elixir, as the ingredients were believed to have profound healing qualities. Whether this is truth or wishful thinking, the drink is both intriguing and tasty.

Ingredients
1 large capon
2 pound fresh or dried dates
2 pounds raisins or currants
1 ounce ground nutmeg
2 ounce ground mace
1 gallon mild ale or dry white wine

The original recipe was far more intense to make in ancient times, and the process would not be appealing today. One would first have crushed the bones of the rooster with the dates and raisins, letting the mixture ferment in the skin of an animal, such as a goat, for several weeks. This animal's skin, simply called sack, gave the drink its name.

Cock Ale

The most common way to make cock ale today is with malt extracts, hops, brown sugar, and yeast, but my recipe is far more simplistic. First cook the capon, either by pan frying with a little sunflower oil or by oven-roasting without herbs or spices. Next, cut the chicken up into small strips and set aside. Using a potato masher or mortar and pestle, mash the raisins or currant berries and dates. Combine the mashed ingredients, spices, and cooked meat in a large pot or fermentation jug. Pour in the ale and let it sit in the refrigerator for 24 hours.

The next day, pour the mixture through a strainer lined with cheesecloth into a separate clean jug. Let it ferment in the refrigerator at least two weeks. Made with a fine, mild ale, the brew will taste like broth. Using dry white wine, it has a more exotic taste with the slightest hint of chicken. Serves 4 to 6.

Yuletide Wassail
ENGLISH RECIPE, CA. SIXTEENTH CENTURY

"Here's to thee, old apple tree; that blooms well, bears well…Hats full, caps full, three bushel bags full, an' all under one tree … Hurrah! Hurrah!"

This quaint ode to the ancient act of wassailing, as collected by the Whimple History Society of East Devon, England, shows the importance of fruit trees to pagan and commoners alike. One of the most favored holiday drinks in the history of antiquated beverages, wassail has been an English tradition for many centuries and continues to usher in jubilant cheer today, though its roots can be traced back to the dark ages. Wassailing, or *waes hael*, a toast to health and prosperity, was a Celtic and Germanic ritual that involved walking through the orchards, singing and drinking to the health of the trees. It both thanked and beseeched the orchard's production in the years to come.

Yuletide Wassail

Wassail is easy to make and will delight your guests during the winter months and all through the year. It gives off the aroma of old England, when the scent of apples filled the air and rolling fog blanketed the countryside, when our ancestors danced and sang in the dark of night, to rejoice the Yuletide season and the winter solstice.

Ingredients
12 cinnamon sticks
1 tablespoon ground allspice
30 to 40 whole cloves
6 cups cider or hard apple juice
3 cups cranberry juice
2 teaspoons aromatic bitters (found in gourmet grocers and liquor stores)
3 small apples, cubed or cut in shards
6 medium juice oranges
2 cups brandy
2 eggs
½ cup raw or natural sugar
5–10 slices of bread (for toast to serve with the drink)
1–2 slices candied fruit for garnish (optional)

Preheat the oven to 325 degrees F., and then crush the cinnamon sticks, allspice, and half of the cloves into pieces using a mortar and pestle. Take the crushed and broken pieces and wrap in a large piece of cheese cloth and tie the ends with string. Take the remainder of the cloves, and pierce them into three of the whole oranges, and three of the apples, and then slice the rest into thin slivers. Next, combine the cider or apple juice, along with the cranberry juice, and aromatic bitters into a stainless steel or glass casserole dish and bake for 30 minutes, making sure not to boil. Stir the mixture to agitate the ingredients, and then add the sachet of spices, and the remaining apples and oranges. After 15 minutes, add the brandy and turn off the heat.

Take the eggs and divide the yolks from the whites. Beat the egg yolks until light, and put aside. In another bowl, whip egg whites until stiff and frothy. Remove the casserole dish from the oven, and set aside. Fold in the egg yolks with the whites, and then slowly pour in about a half cup of the wassail to the egg mixture, slowly stirring in order to temper it. Remove the spice sachet from the wassail and pour in the egg mixture. Transfer to a punch bowl if you wish, or leave in the hot dish. Float the baked apple and orange slices in the wassail and ladle to each mug, topping each mug with a small slice of toast if desired, to represent the ancient custom of offering.

This wonderful drink will not only lift the spirits of your guests, but will add a special scent to your home that will pronounce to all that good times are waiting inside, inviting everyone who catches the delightful aroma, that a celebrative occasion awaits. Offer bread for dipping and place the moist bread in the boughs of trees as was done in ancient times, to offer prosperity and hope for the year ahead. Serves 15 to 20.

Raisin Stepony Wine
ENGLISH RECIPE CA. SIXTEENTH CENTURY

This simple recipe, with its unique flavor of raisins or currants, creates an atmospheric drink that was widely enjoyed during Elizabethan times and readily found in public eating houses, enjoyed by soldier, sailor, and commoner alike. It is said to have been mentioned in the diary of several sailors under the command of Sir Francis Drake and during the English occupation of Saint Augustine, Florida, of the seventeenth century.

Making a good Stepony wine requires less work than one might think, but will take some time, so you may wish to prepare this beverage several weeks ahead of time.

Ingredients
1 gallon of distilled water
1 pound of raisins or currants
1 pound raw or natural sugar
2 large lemons
1 ounce powdered ginger

Pour the distilled water into a large stainless steel or glass pot and heat to medium-high. In separate dish, mash the raisins, currants, or both until pulverized. Add these to the water, and then add the sugar and stir, making sure it does not boil. Add the lemon juice to the mixture; cover and let simmer for 30 to 40 minutes.

Thinly slice the lemon peels and set aside. Once the raisin mixture has cooked down, turn off the heat and cool. When cool, strain the mixture into an earthenware pot, adding the sliced lemon peel. Cover and let set for three or four days in the refrigerator. Discard the peel and return to the refrigerator for several weeks. When ready, remove any froth, strain into dark-colored bottles, and chill. Serve in wine goblets or small tankards chilled or at room temperature. Offer with stout cheeses or sweet desserts for the best pairing. Servings vary.

Raisin Stepony Wine

Syllabub
ENGLISH/FRENCH RECIPE, CA. SEVENTEENTH CENTURY

The traditional syllabub drink is believed to have originated in the Sillery region of France somewhere during the early part of the seventeenth century. The English slang word bub refers to a frothy or bubbling drink found in taverns and public houses throughout the British Isles. This drink goes nicely with sweet desserts and candied fruit, as the dry palate balances well together and aids digestion after big meals.

Syllabub

Ingredients
½ cup Madeira wine
½ cup dry white wine
2 cups heavy whipping cream
½ cup natural or white sugar
1 lemon, juice and zest
1 teaspoon ground nutmeg

In a large pitcher or punch bowl, mix in the Madeira, white wine, whipping cream, and sugar and whisk until the cream begins to stiffen. Fold in the lemon juice and zest, then ladle into medium-sized dessert or parfait glasses and chill at least an hour before serving, garnishing with nutmeg. As the wine mixture and cream separates, this drink will become a favorite at your parties.

Another historical favorite is brandy syllabub, a warming drink that was fashionable with noble and commoner alike. Much like the previous dessert drink, brandy syllabub makes a wonderful after-dinner drink and goes well with desserts.

Ingredients
1 cup dry white wine
¼ to 1 cup brandy
2 cups heavy whipping cream
¼ cup white sugar
2 tablespoons lemon juice
1 tablespoon orange zest (optional)

Mix together the white wine, brandy, whipping cream, and sugar, stirring until the sugar is dissolved and the cream begins to stiffen. Fold in the grated orange peel, then ladle the mixture into medium-sized dessert or parfait glasses and chill at least an hour before serving. Sprinkle on the remaining orange zest for taste and appearance. Note that you may also wish to use apricot brandy instead of regular brandy to add an exotic flavor. Serves 8.

Raspberry Shrub

ENGLISH RECIPE, CA. SEVENTEENTH CENTURY

Here's an easy recipe that was highly regarded by the nobility during the English reign of the New World, and that continues to please modern folks world-wide. Although there are variations to the traditional shrub recipe, this particular libation is believed to have been common to the men of the Golden Hind and Sir Francis Drake during their historic travels through the Americas, and was a favorite drink in taverns everywhere. Remember that this recipe is formulated as a concentrate to be added to water, though you may also add it to fresh fruit juices, such as blackberry, elderberry, or blueberry juice, or even a fine rosé wine for extra body.

Raspberry Shrub

Ingredients
2 pounds fresh raspberries
1½ cups apple cider vinegar
3 cups raw or natural sugar
Water or rosé wine (add two parts to
    each glass)

In a large earthen crock or jug, mix together the raspberries and apple cider vinegar. With a potato masher, crush the berry and vinegar mixture to a mush, cover with wax paper, and secure tightly with string. Let the mixture rest in a cool, dark place, or your refrigerator, for at least two weeks. When ready, place the mixture in a pot and bring to a boil. Reduce to medium-low heat, stirring constantly, while adding the sugar. Continue to cook and stir for 30 minutes. While still hot, strain the mixture, then pour the liquid into colored bottles, cork, and refrigerate. When ready to serve, add one part shrub mixture to two parts cold water or rosé wine. Mix and serve with a few raspberries or mint leaves.

Cornish Ginger Wine

ENGLISH RECIPE, CA. SIXTEENTH CENTURY

One of my favorite wines, this recipe is believed to have originated around the time of the Roman occupancy of the ancient Britons. There are several variations of this base recipe, including the use of honey, cowslip flowers, damson, blackberry, rhubarb, elderberry, and ginger, which would have been brought in by trade ships and was used to settle the stomach, warm the body, and help circulation. In the Dark Ages and medieval times, many Cornish countrymen and women would have enjoyed this drink during a feast or village celebration, especially during the winter months, as it would warm the stomach and prepare one for a hearty meal. It was also a choice wine for the autumn solstice, as its color denoted the season and offered reassurance that they would survive the winter ahead.

Cornish Ginger Wine

Ingredients
2 gallons spring water
10 cups of raw or refined sugar
1 large ginger root (peeled, washed, and sliced thin)
12 lemons
½ cup red currants or raisins
3 ounces fresh yeast
1 pint brandy

In a large glass or stainless steel pot, bring the water to a boil, adding the sugar while stirring. Add the ginger and gently boil or 20 minutes. Peel and slice the lemons into ½-inch slices and set aside. Add the rinds to the mixture, and then turn off heat and let cool. When cool, add the lemon slices and red currants and stir. Add the yeast, stirring until dissolved. Once mixed, add the liquid to clean wine bottles, or to make the finished product look truly authentic, use glass demijohns or carboys to store and serve from. Let the mixture rest in the refrigerator on its side and with a cork in it for at least a month so that it can ferment properly. When ready, add the brandy, and pour through a sieve or cheesecloth into clean wine bottles, and serve chilled. Serves 5 to 8.

Metheglin (Cornish Ginger Mead)

ENGLISH RECIPE, CA. ELEVENTH CENTURY

Metheglin is likely one of the oldest drinks found in Cornwall and Wales, and also one of the easiest, because it did not require sugar to brew. Believed to have found its way from Scandinavia during the Viking raids centuries before, it was a favorite drink thought to heal the body. Metheglin is light, yet hearty, offering a sweet drink with a little kick. This is yet another libation perfect for the winter months or at fall celebrations like the autumn solstice or Yuletide.

Ingredients
1 gallon of spring water
3 cups natural honey (flower or clover is good)
1 large honeycomb
1 large ginger root (peeled, washed and sliced)
1 ounce active yeast

Metheglin Ginger Mead

In a large saucepan or pot, pour the water over the honeycomb and honey, cover with wax paper, tie with string to make sure it's relatively airtight, and let sit for at least two weeks in the refrigerator or in a cool, dark place. In ancient times, this would not have been necessary in the English countryside because it was usually cool year-round, but to keep bugs out, we will use a cool, airtight place like a refrigerator.

When ready, stir well, and then strain the liquid into another clean saucepan and bring to a light boil. Place the ginger into a cheesecloth or muslin bag and bruise with a rolling pin or wood mallet. Add the tied bag of bruised ginger root to the boiling liquid and simmer on low heat for two to three hours. When done, remove from heat and let cool until slightly warm. Remove foam or froth from the liquid and add the yeast. Stir until well-mixed and let cool. Pour the liquid into clean wine bottles or use glass demijohns or colored carboys to store the wine. Serve chilled in wide wine goblets. Serves 4 to 6.

"The staff of life, the cure for strife—"All sorrows are less with bread." —Miguel de Cervantes Saavedra (1547–1616)

"Caxton Dinner" from William Caxton's *The Canterbury Tales*, circa 1484. *Courtesy of Society for Creative Anachronism, Arts and Sciences of the Middle Ages and Renaissance*

Since man's discovery of grains, breads and ground meal have been the staple of the European diet. From nobility to the common folk, bread was likely the most important food for everyday life, though how people ate it, and how often they would get to eat it, was vastly different. Simple dark breads were the most popular, especially for the poor, and white and lighter breads were usually reserved for the wealthy. As our ancient relatives began to migrate, they carried with them as much of the vital grain-seed as possible, and it was understood that doing so meant their very lives. Although American soil was different from the moist grounds of England and most of Europe, and the arid farmlands of Spain and the Mediterranean, colonists reproduced certain farming conditions to grow new crops. The food that graced the tables of their families across the seas followed them, in all its tasty glory.

Once in the Americas, bread was limited, as seed supplies were slim. Until they were able to bring in fertile crops of wheat and barley, the colonists lived off the corn introduced by the native Indians. Dark breads continued to be the bread of the poor, and throughout most of the sixteenth century many were forced to add corn husks, wheat chaff, and even sawdust to make the bread full and robust. Sadly, many of these darker grains had molds and funguses that had a hallucinogenic effect on those who ate it. In fact, contemporary archaeologists now believe that a common fungus known as ergot may have been partially responsible for many panic outbreaks, such as the European inquisition and the Salem witch trials.

The following recipes are both simple to prepare and wonderful to eat. Each is historically accurate, though the baking method is different. The colonists used large hearth ovens, and without simple forms of yeast, the consistency was tougher. Though the recipes date back to the Crusades, most are still enjoyed in Europe today. Try these breads fresh from the oven with a little butter mixed with herbs and spices or with rich butter and honey. Enjoy them with the hearty soup and stew recipes that follow.

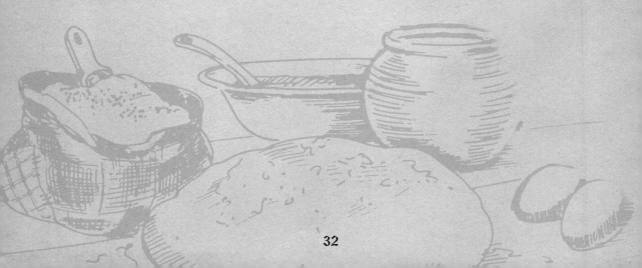

Trencher Meal Bread

EUROPEAN RECIPE, CA. FOURTEENTH CENTURY

Trencher bread is an ancient food dating from about the eleventh century. Though the term was used for wooden plates that served noble and peasant alike, similar to the cafeteria trays we know today, there was also a popular bread of the same name that was used as an edible plate. It held many kinds of foods, including stews, thick soups and beef with thick gravies. After a noble feast, the bread plate was often given to the poor as penitence to the church. Since this historically accurate recipe is still used today, it stands to reason

Trencher Meal Bread

that our Paganus ancestors enjoyed trencher bread often. Enjoy this bread both as an offering to the earth, and for the harvest year as thanks for your prosperity and blessings.

Ingredients
1¾ cups warm water, divided
5 tablespoons clover honey
2 packages active dry yeast
8 cups unbleached flour, divided
6 large eggs, plus 1 egg yolk
2 tablespoons sea salt
2/3 cup currants (optional)
7 tablespoons whole butter, softened
2 tablespoons ground cinnamon
2 tablespoons dried basil
2½ tablespoons dried rosemary (powdered
½ cup finely chopped fresh parsley (optional)

Preheat the oven to 375 degrees F.

Pour half of the warm water into a large bowl and add the honey. Stir well, add the yeast, stir, and let sit for 5 minutes. Pour in the rest of the warm water and slowly scoop in 3 cups of flour, mixing all ingredients well with a wooden spoon. Cover with a damp cloth or towel and let sit for 45 minutes. In a separate bowl, beat 5 of the eggs and add the sea salt, currants, and softened butter. Beat until well mixed and let sit for at least 45 minutes. When the dough has at least doubled in size, add the spices, dried herbs, fresh parsley, and egg mixture, and fold with the wooden spoon.

Add the remaining 5 cups of flour and stir until well blended, then knead with your hands for at least 10 minutes, adding flour as needed. Place in a bowl and cover with the damp cloth again. Let this sit in a warm place for about 1 hour. After that, knead the dough again and turn over, cover, and let rest for another 30 minutes. Form the dough into two separate balls and place on a floured board, patting each into two long rolls. Beat the egg yolk until frothy, add cinnamon, and brush over the loaves. Place on a buttered cookie sheet and bake for 35 to 45 minutes or until golden brown. Cool on a rack. Serve whole or cut down the middle and serve with warm herb butter. Or offer it as a bowl to your guests, tearing out the top to hold stews and thick soups. Serves 4 to 6.

Manchet Bread
ENGLISH/FRENCH RECIPE, CA. FOURTEENTH CENTURY

Dating at least to the fourteenth century, traditional manchet bread was as commonplace as mead or wine in its day, and could be served as a meal itself if necessary. This particular recipe is one you can use any time and is a wonderful addition to the soups and pottages in this book.

Ingredients
3 cups white or dark wheat flour
4 tablespoons butter
1¼ cups lukewarm water
1 tablespoon yeast
1 tablespoon sugar
½ tablespoon salt
3 eggs (for brushing)
whole oats (for dusting, optional)

Preheat the oven to 350 degrees F.

In a large mixing bowl, combine all the ingredients and mix with a fork or electric mixer. To save time, you may wish to use a bread machine. Each batch should be formed into three separate loaves, wrapped loosely in cheesecloth or wax

Manchet Bread and Stilton cheese

paper, and set to rise for 1 to 2 hours. You may wish to place them in the refrigerator for a day, or even overnight. Before baking, beat the eggs until foamy, and brush liberally over each loaf. Place on a greased baking sheet and bake for 35 minutes or until golden brown. Manchet was often a flat, round bread served warm with jams, honey, or melted butter. If you wish to make the dough in advance, simply cover the cheesecloth-wrapped dough with tin foil and freeze. Serves 6 to 8.

English Bisket

ENGLISH RECIPE, CA. SEVENTEENTH CENTURY

These biscuits have lingered through history since medieval times, and across the seas to Jamestown and beyond. For sailor or soldier, they would fare well on journeys, becoming hard as crackers but remaining edible for long periods of time. English biskets are likely one of the richest breads in history, and this recipe reflects a time when no one cared about calories, fats, and carbohydrates. So, be warned! You may enjoy this marvelous bisket without an ounce of guilt.

Ingredients
24 egg yolks
1 tablespoon anise extract
1 cup aniseeds, finely crushed and bruised
1 tablespoon standard yeast
2½ sticks whole butter, softened
1 quart heavy cream
8 cups or 4 pounds wheat flour
½ cup raw sugar

Preheat oven to 400 degrees F.

Mix together the egg yolks, aniseed extract, aniseeds, and yeast. Add the butter, cream, and wheat flower and mix until the dough is paste-like. Form small flattened balls, lay them on butcher's brown paper or wax paper, and bake 5 to 8 minutes, until the dough has slightly risen. Take the biskets out and let them cool slightly before your feast. Just before your gathering, you may rub brown sugar over the biskets and return them to the oven for 10 minutes, or until golden brown. These biskets are wonderful served warm and with honey, and are perfect for breakfast or supper. Serves around 20.

English Bisket with honey and spice butter

Diar Seed Bread

ENGLISH/WELSH RECIPE CA. FOURTEENTH CENTURY

Diar bread is one of the heartiest breads of ancient times. Used for a number of reasons, from religious occasions to a simple staple for the common meal, diar bread has passed through history with great reverence. Diar bread is commonly a wheat or rye bread with caraway seeds and made much like manchet, so it's a rather simplistic recipe, yet works well with a mix of herbs such as rosemary and sage, or with thyme, parsley, and salt, offering a rich and fulfilling taste suitable with any meal.

During the plagues, it was a common gift to those suffering, as the herbs or seeds were thought to aid the sick. For Paganus peoples across the English Isles, this bread, along with cheese and a dark wine, would serve as a nightly meal during the summer solstice, as it was believed that the heartiness of the bread would give strength for the next day in the fields. Offer this bread warm with a shard of cheese, and leave on a plate for the spirits of the dead during Samhain as a respectful gesture.

Diar Seed Bread with cheddar and mushrooms

Ingredients
1¼ cups lukewarm water
3 cups wheat flour
1 tablespoons yeast
1 tablespoons sugar
5 tablespoons whole caraway or sesame seeds
½ tablespoon salt
3 egg yolks (for brushing only)

Preheat oven to 375 degrees F.

Combine all the ingredients in a large bowl and mix with an electric mixer or fork. You may wish to use a bread machine for kneading and to aid the initial rising of the dough. Form the dough into three loaves, then loosely wrap each in cheesecloth or wax paper and set to rise for 30 to 60 minutes. You may wish to place them in the refrigerator for a day, or even overnight. Before baking, beat the eggs until foamy and brush over the loaves. Place on a greased baking sheet and bake for 35 minutes or until golden brown.

Another way to serve diar bread is to toast it in butter on a grill or iron skillet until crisp. You may substitute dried raisins or currants for the seeds in the dough, or use spices like cinnamon or nutmeg to make Yuletide bread, which is always a hit when wassailing with friends, and it also works well for French toast!

Winter Fest Squash Muffins
ENGLISH RECIPE, CA. SIXTEENTH CENTURY

Although the native squash was not introduced in Europe until the early sixteenth century, by the colonial period many settlers were growing the hearty squash. Of course, the ancient Indians were harvesting various types of squash centuries before the Europeans arrived. This early eighteenth-century recipe from Salem, Massachusetts, is both fun to make and delicious. Serve these at your winter solstice gatherings to speed winter and welcome spring.

Winter Fest Squash Muffins

Ingredients
2½ cups white flour
¼ teaspoon sea salt
1 teaspoon cream of tartar
1½ teaspoons baking powder
½ teaspoon baking soda
1 cup sweet whole milk
  (add 3 tablespoons sugar)
1 cup cooked winter squash, such as
  acorn squash
1 tablespoon butter, softened or melted
½ cup raw or natural sugar
zest of 1 orange (optional)

Pre-heat oven to 400 degrees F.

Prepare 2 muffin pans, preferably with natural paper cups. In a large bowl, combine the flour, salt, cream of tartar, baking powder, and baking soda and mix well, making sure the dry ingredients are well sifted. Add the sweetened milk, and then mix in the shredded squash, butter, and sugar with a large spoon until a thick paste forms. Add the flour and stir until nicely moist. If you like, add the orange zest, then pour the mixture into the pans and bake for 20 minutes. The orange zest was popular in the southern American colonies and throughout the coastal regions of the new world. If you decide not to use the orange zest, dish up these wonderful muffins hot and with fresh ginger or orange preserves to make a delightfully authentic treat. Serves 6 to 8.

Welsh Cakes
WELSH RECIPE, CA. SEVENTEENTH CENTURY

Welsh cakes go by the names Apple Dragon, Newport Lovely, Bakestones, or Jam Split, suggestive of J. R. R. Tolkien's Hobbiton or something you might snack on while visiting the Green Dragon Inn. In the proper Welsh-Gaelic languages of Cymraeg or y Gymraeg, the names sound no less adventurous: *Pice ar y maen* and *Llech Cymraeg* make one think of far-off lands, dragons, and trolls.

Welsh Cakes with fresh berries

These wonderful little gems are reminiscent of early public houses that dotted the English countryside. Though they are a Welsh and Cornish recipe, the delightful cakes greeted cold, hungry travelers at inns or public houses as they waited for their meal. This recipe was discovered in the journal of a mid-seventeenth-century baker, when Cavaliers and Roundheads battled in the nearby moors and forests for domination of the crown. Welsh cakes would have been popular with commoner and noble alike and have survived the centuries to remain a popular and honored dish in my ancestors' homeland. Different from typical pancakes or griddle cakes, they could be served hot or cold and could have been accompanied by fruits, jams, and tea.

Ingredients
8 ounces self-rising flour
4 ounces sugar (castor, or superfine, sugar is best)
1 pinch sea salt
5 ounces butter, softened
1 egg
2 tablespoons whole milk
2 ounces currants, blueberries, or sultanas (optional)
2–3 slices butter for grilling
½ cup powdered sugar (for dusting)

In a medium-sized bowl, sift the flour, sugar, and salt together, and rub in the butter. Whisk in the egg, milk and seasonal berries (optional). Knead the dough until firm. On a floured surface, roll out to about ¼-inch thick. Cut into 3-inch circles, or simply use a biscuit cutter, and then place each in a hot skillet and cook on both sides until golden. If you want a less filling texture, add ½ cup milk to the batter. This will make them lighter and more like pancakes. Dab each with a little butter, dust with sugar, and serve hot. Serves 12 to 15.

"My salad days—When I was green in judgment."
—William Shakespeare (1564–1616)

The Shepherd's Great Calendar, ca. fifteenth century. *Courtesy of Society for Creative Anachronism,*

It might amaze us to know that our ancestors would have enjoyed a fresh salad of tossed green leaves and herbs as much as we do today. There is evidence that even before the Middle Ages, Europeans enjoyed a wide variety of salads, although rather unique examples of what we would consider a salad today. The French and Mediterranean cultures may be among the first to have taken advantage of the earth's vegetative bounty, where all fruits, herbs, and vegetables were used to create lavish culinary delights or simple meals. Our ancestors would most likely have taken their salad at the end of the meal with a dark wine as an aid to digest their food, which could be rich and bloating.

Dark and rich leaves and vegetables would have been the primary ingredients in a common salad, though grain salads were also common. Bulgur wheat, spelt, and kamut grains, as well as wheat berries and barley mixed with honey or milk would have made a filling dish when meats were off the menu. In some instances; especially for the wealthy, imported fruits from the Mediterranean made scrumptious salads that would show up even the most robust dishes. Made with melons, peaches, grapes and various nuts, and mixed with honey and a zesty lemon wine known as Mosxato, kings and queens would have favored this salad. Likewise, when citrus fruits such as oranges, breadfruit, lemons, and limes became a delicacy in the courts, salad became something nourishing and exotic. With such fruits available to the early colonists, it stands to reason that the innovative cook would have taken advantage of these delights.

The salad recipes included here have been taken from actual records and literature of earlier periods and can be made with little effort. Sauces and dressings, although used in many cultures, are an addition best left up to the reader. If you would like to add a little zest to your salad, please refer to the Sauces and Vinegars section of this book.

Folk Herb Salat
FRENCH/ENGLISH RECIPE CA. SIXTEENTH CENTURY

Salads made of herbs and greens were commonplace throughout ancient times. By the colonial period, many people would take the salad, or *salat,* before a great meal with bread and butter. This Folk Herb Salat recipe dates to the medieval period and would have been on the tables of noble and the middle classes alike, and served in various ways and with different sauces depending upon the occasion. Though such salads would change greatly according to the season and what was growing in the herb garden, most salads like this were simple creations and readily available throughout the year.

Folk Herb Salat with Claret wine

Ingredients
2 bunches watercress
1 bunch spinach, thinly sliced
6 spring onions or scallions, finely chopped
1 fennel bulb, thinly sliced
1 to 3 leeks, thinly sliced
1 handful of fresh parsley
1 sprig fresh rosemary
4–8 sprigs fresh mint, finely chopped
6 fresh sage leaves
2 branches thyme
pinch of sea salt
black pepper, freshly ground
2–3 tablespoons red wine Vinegar
4–5 tablespoons olive oil

Wash the watercress and herbs, and then hand-dry thoroughly. Mix in the herbs, leeks, and onions in a large bowl with a dash of salt and pepper. In a small dish, combine the oil with the vinegar, add more salt and pepper to taste, and pour over the salad before serving. Dish up on flat plates and serve with warm manchet bread and freshly mixed herb butter.

Salet of Lemmones (Lemon Salad)

LEMON SALAD RECIPE CA. SEVENTEENTH TO EIGHTEENTH CENTURY

As with many recipes of the ancient world, a good portion of the fruits later seen in the English Isles and Europe would have come from abroad, often as gifts from foreign dignitaries or monks on pilgrimages. Quince and citrus would have been a delicacy of great price, and a proper lemon was certainly among these commodities. Hailing from Sorrento and the Amalfi Coast of Italy, these beautiful lemons have a tangy flavor without the overpowering tartness. Popular throughout the Middle Ages and well into the Elizabethan era, this recipe works exceedingly well with fish and meat dishes and sweet cheeses.

Salet of Lemmones with a chardonnay and sugar

Ingredients
4–6 large Meyer lemons
6 tablespoons raw sugar
½ cup fresh basil, minced
zest of one orange (for Elizabethan-
    period recipes)

Wash and dry the lemons and orange, and then peel a thin layer of the lemon with a vegetable peeler so that the lemon takes on a light yellow hue. Slice thinly and remove all the seeds. Arrange the lemon slices on a platter. Sprinkle the fresh basil over each slice and garnish with small flowers or herbs. Offer with a bowl of coarse, raw sugar for sprinkling and dipping, and consider serving a dry white wine. Serves 4 to 6.

Herbe Salat (Mixed Herb Salad)

FRENCH/ENGLISH RECIPE CA. SIXTEENTH CENTURY

This traditional recipe was a common salad found in many banquet and court meals. Favored by the wealthy and commoner alike, this dish would often be as elaborately dressed as the dining room it was served in. With flowers and herbs displayed like a work of art, this salad will be sure to receive many compliments.

Finding fresh flowers that haven't been sprayed with insecticides may be difficult, however. Look for a wholesale organic herb farm or nursery that specializes in edible flowers.

4 hard boiled eggs, sliced thick
1 small head of butter lettuce
1 cup chopped watercress
½ cup fresh flower petals (optional)
1 cucumber, lightly peeled and sliced
4 tablespoons olive oil
3 tablespoons white wine vinegar
½–1 tablespoon sea salt
freshly ground pepper to taste
½ tablespoon brown sugar
¼ cup fresh tarragon leaves
¼ cup fresh mint leaves

Herbe Salat with Cheddar and Manchet bread

Boil the eggs and cool in water while preparing the salad. Wash the lettuce and watercress in cold water, dry with a paper towel, and refrigerate. Gently rinse the flower petals in cold water, dry, and refrigerate. Rip the lettuce into small sections and mix with the watercress, transferring into a large salad bowl or serving platter. Place the cucumbers around the edge of the bowl or platter to resemble a flower. Do the same with the thickly sliced eggs, and then sprinkle the flower petals over the lettuce and watercress mix.

Mix the oil and vinegar and pour over the salad just before serving. If you like, sprinkle brown sugar over the entire salad and garnish with tarragon and mint leaves. Serves 4 to 6.

Watercress and Violet Salat

ENGLISH/FRENCH RECIPE CA. SIXTEENTH CENTURY

This salad was a popular choice for the royals and would have been seen in modest homes during the Renaissance. Today, salads that contain violets, violas, and pansies are not only viewed as edible but also as being quite healthy, as they are loaded with phytochemicals and medicinal constituents now believed to aid in tissue regeneration, and even help to cure certain diseases. This salad's delicate flavor and color give it a unique and authentic appeal. Remember, it is important to only purchase fresh flowers that have not been sprayed with insecticides or other chemicals. Organic is always best.

Watercress and Violet Salat and cheese and bread

Ingredients
2 bunches watercress, washed and separated
2 cups violets or violas, washed and de-stemmed
1 cup pansies, washed and de-stemmed
4 tablespoons white wine vinegar
4 tablespoons olive oil
½–1 tablespoon sea salt
freshly ground pepper to taste
½ tablespoons brown sugar

Wash the watercress in cold water, dry, and refrigerate. Gently rinse the attached flower petals in cold water, dry, and refrigerate separately. When ready to serve, transfer to a large salad bowl or serving platter and sprinkle the flower petals over the watercress, then pour the oil and vinegar lightly over all just before serving. Sprinkle with salt, pepper, and brown sugar to taste. This recipe goes great with warm diar bread and soft herbal butter. Serves 4 to 6.

Parsley, Onion, and Sage Salade
FRENCH/ENGLISH RECIPE CA. SIXTEENTH CENTURY

A favorite salad dating to the Dark Ages, this recipe served as a meal when food was scarce and when illness was rampant. Onions and garlic were thought to be healing vegetables. Their fiery taste would heat the system and warm the palate. This is a simple dish to prepare, and hearty enough to work with any meal. As onions of various types are known to grow in almost any field, it's easy to see why this recipe was so popular in desperate times.

Parsley, Onion, and Sage Salade with cheese

Ingredients
2 medium onions
1–3 large shallots, sliced thin
1 bunch parsley, coarsely chopped
1 bunch basil, finely chopped
2–4 cloves garlic, sliced thin
½ cup red wine vinegar

Chop the onions, shallots, parsley, and basil into small pieces. Slice the garlic cloves into thin slivers and place together in a large bowl, preferably an earthen pie dish. Add the red wine vinegar and mix. Refrigerate for an hour or two before your meal, allowing the flavors to meld. You may wish to serve on small plates along with warm bread, such as manchet, or in place of plates—serve the salad with warm trencher meal bread so your guests can enjoy their salad on an edible plate. If you like, you may add fresh tomatoes and wedges of cheese to liven up this dish, which would have been done in Elizabethan cooking, and offer a small bowl of vinegar to brighten the flavors. Serves 4 to 6.

Chapter 4. Pottages, Soups, and Festive Hors d'oeuvres

"The discovery of a new dish does more for the happiness of the human race than the discovery of a star." —Jean Anthelme Brillat-Savarin (1755–1856)

Cook working in Kitchen, by Hans Burgkmair, ca. sixteenth century. *Courtesy of Society for Creative Anachronism, Arts and Sciences of the Middle Ages and Renaissance*

Soups, stews, and appetizers were an important staple throughout Europe's ancient history, so it stands to reason that such time-honored dishes would find their way across the land and oceans. For the Paganus folk of 500 years ago, a highly flavored morsel of braised beef resting on a wedge of toasted bread or a thick stew and simple bread would have been a blessing. Yet on the high holidays and special occasions, the villagers would often pull their resources together and make a feast.

The ancients would have used what they had to make the celebration festive. During Imbolc, for instance, braised bacon and boiled or creamed leeks, curried lamb, soups, and braided breads would have been common. A Beltane celebration would have brought out the oat bannocks, roasted capon stews, field beans, fertility breads, and boiled eggs, and Yule might include an ancient Roman dish of Gianciale, the roasted jowl of pig, as well as wildfowl and venison. Each celebration would signify what a holiday stood for and why such foods were important to them. We might think our ancestors ate bland and boring foods, tasteless breads and cheeses, and flavorless drinks. And, though it might have been difficult, our ancestors were innovative, to say the least. They could turn a bland shank of meat or salted fish into something exciting and delicious.

As an opening statement to a feast or as a feast unto itself, what you serve is entirely up to you. Many of my friends and colleagues serve libations and hors d'oeuvres first, as a way to welcome their guests and offer polite salutations to the gathering, while the pottages, soups, and breads are served with the main course. This is usually done in potluck or family-style fashion and is always a winner. There are no rules, simply that you find the expression that works best for you. There could be many diverse and exotic stews and soups that express your distinct lineage and honor your ancestors. As my lineage follows the Welsh, pan-Celtic, and Scandinavian tribes, there are many foods that represent me. I could offer a Welsh stew known as cawl, a thick combination of meats and vegetables like many stews throughout Europe. You may wish to add warm breads, butters, compotes, and preserves along with an assortment of hors d'oeuvres to draw in the crowd and tantalize your guest's palate for the feast to come.

The majority of these recipes had been discovered in fourteen- to seventeenth-century cookbooks in academic and national museum collections today. They represent some of the most common and beloved foods of our ancestors. For presentation, you may wish to use authentic-looking bowls and large wooden or metal platters lined with roughage to ground the atmosphere with the old and time-honored, giving your gathering a kind of respect that hasn't been seen in centuries.

Funge Pasties (Sweet and Spicy Mushroom Pasties)

FRENCH RECIPE CA. FOURTEENTH CENTURY

According to the *Le Menagier de Paris*, or The Goodman of Paris, ca. 1393: "Mushrooms of one night are the best and they are little and red within and closed at the top . . . Peeled and then washed in hot water, parboiled and put into a pasty with oil, cheese, and Poudre Fort. . . Place betwixt two dishes on the coals, and then add salt and cheese."

The following recipe sounds more difficult than it is, and these little tarts will be the life of your event. Serve these little delicacies with a well-balanced dark red wine or hearty ale.

Ingredients
1 pound fresh mushrooms (The best varieties for this recipe are golden or black chanterelle and morels, though large button mushrooms work just as well.)
5 tablespoons extra virgin olive oil or grapeseed oil
½ pound provolone cheese, grated coarsely
1 teaspoon powder fort (see appendix)
½ cup French Cantal or any triple crème cheese
salt to taste

For the pastry dough:
¾ cup unsalted butter
3 cup all-purpose flour
1½ teaspoons sea salt
12 tablespoons water
1 tablespoon lard or baking grease (for pan)

Cut the butter into tablespoon-size slices and let soften until ready to use. Sift the flour and salt together in a large bowl. Cut in the butter until well blended. Add half the water and mix it into the flour mixture to make pliable dough. Form the dough into a ball, wrap in wax paper, and refrigerate for at least an hour.

Preheat the oven to 400 degrees F.

Knead the dough on a floured board for roughly 5 minutes, adding flour if the dough is too sticky, or water if it is too dry. Roll the dough into a flat, round shape about ½-inch thick and cut into 5-inch squares. Place the square on a plate, cover with wax paper, and refrigerate until ready to use.

Stem the mushrooms and chop coarsely. Place in a medium-sized saucepan with a little oil and saute for about 20 minutes. Drain the mushrooms, then stir in the grated cheese, olive or grapeseed oil, and powder fort and set aside to cool. At this point, you can follow one of two methods. The first is to grease a non-stick mini-muffin tin with the lard or cooking grease and line each cup with the dough. This should make 48 tarts. Spoon the mushroom filling into each cup, but do not overfill. Cover each tart with the remaining dough and pinch closed. The second method is simpler. Spoon the mushroom mixture onto the dough squares and fold, then crimp the edges with a fork.

Bake 15 to 20 minutes, until lightly brown. Dole out the Cantal cheese or triple crème cheese into a small, decorated bowl and serve with pâté knives, along with your powder fort box for a little extra spice. Serves 8 to 10.

Funge Pasties and Cock Ale

Pompys (Medieval Meatballs in Sweet Sauce)

ENGLISH RECIPE, CA. FIFTEENTH CENTURY

Pompys (pronounced pum-pees) is likely one of the first meatball dishes seen in Western Europe, specifically in the British Isles. This recipe, based on one in a fifteenth-century cookbook, is an authentic example of a common hors d'oeuvre of the Middles Ages. It is as succulent as a modern-day meatball, but uniquely sweet and spicy, a notable hallmark of the ancient world. It is simple to make and appropriate for any event, especially when serving a large crowd. Serve these sweet and spicy little meatballs from a large platter, smothered in sauce, or with the sauce served in small bowls on a bed of roughage.

Pompys with olives, field vegetables, and white wine

Ingredients
2 cups beef broth
½ cup red wine
1 pound beef (coarsely ground)
1 pound veal (coarsely ground)
3 egg yolks
1½ tablespoon raw or natural sugar
¼ teaspoon ground mace
¼ teaspoon ground cloves
¼ teaspoon ground pepper
¼ teaspoon cinnamon
½ cup red currants or chopped raisins

Sauce:
1 cup mulberries or blackberries (mashed to pulp)
2 cups almond milk
1 tablespoon rice flour
3 tablespoons raw or natural sugar
⅛ teaspoon mace
⅛ teaspoon cinnamon
1 cup mashed mulberries or blackberries (optional)
4 to 6 strands saffron

Place the broth and wine in a pot or deep saucepan, bring to a rolling boil, and reduce heat to medium. In a large bowl, mix the ground beef and veal, along with the egg yolks, sugar, spices, and diced currants or raisins. Form the mixture into balls around 2 inches thick. Spoon into the broth mixture and cook for 15 to 20 minutes until the meat is a dark gray color. Remove the meatballs with a slotted spoon and place in a serving dish, preferably an earthen dish, and let sit.

Make the sauce: In another saucepan, mix together the mashed berries, almond milk, rice flour, sugar, mace, and cinnamon and bring to a soft boil, and then reduce heat to simmer until the mixture is thick and creamy. Dole over the pompys just until you can see half of the meat, sprinkle the saffron over all, and serve steaming hot. Offer this dish with warm bread and herbal butter. Serves 4 to 8.

English Creamed Nut Soup
ENGLISH RECIPE, CA. FOURTEENTH CENTURY

Soups made from nuts and seeds have been popular in Europe since at least the eleventh century. Whether aboard the vessels of the Spanish armada or in the cargo holds of Sir Francis Drake's ships, barrels and barrels of assorted European nuts could fill the ballast. Needless to say, this recipe would have been popular for noble and commoner alike, and could be as filling as a cut of meat.

Although this recipe is similar to Crème Almaundys, a thin broth enjoyed by the French and Spanish, the English version would have had a larger variety of nuts and seeds, sometimes changing with the season's yield.

English Creamed Nut Soup with fresh Diar Seed Bread, sage leaves, and Cock Ale

Ingredients
1 stick butter
1 cup white flour
5 cups chicken stock
12 ounces whole milk
5 ounces almonds, ground fine
5 ounces walnuts, ground fine
3 ounces hazelnuts, ground fine
½ cup heavy cream
1 egg yolk
½ teaspoon ground nutmeg (for sprinkling)
salt and pepper, to taste

In a large saucepan, melt the butter and sprinkle in the flour, and then cook on medium heat for 2 minutes. While stirring, add the chicken stock and milk, and bring to a light boil. Reduce to low and simmer for 15 minutes, stirring constantly. Stir in the ground nuts and simmer for 60 minutes, stirring occasionally. When ready to serve, beat the egg yolk and heavy cream together, and then whisk over high heat for about 5 minutes. Ladle into bowls and sprinkle with nutmeg, salt, and pepper. Offer with warm bread or sweet squash muffins and soft butter, and a dry white wine or stout ale.

Herbe Broth with Eggs and Cheese
ENGLISH RECIPE CA. SIXTEENTH CENTURY

Here's another delightful dish popular during the Tudor age, though it can be traced back to the Roman era. Though there appears to be variations to this broth, as several base broths can be used, a hearty broth made with peas was quite common. This filling soup can be served for the morning, mid-day, or evening meal. Served on bread or as a side dish, it goes well with a meat dish like mutton, beef, or chicken.

Ingredients
3 tablespoons parsley
½ cup grated cheese
3 tablespoons powdered sage
several threads saffron, rubbed or
    powdered
2 cups green pea stock (crushed early
    peas in liquid)
2 cups dry white wine
½ tablespoon ginger
4 to 6 eggs
4 thin slices white bread such as Manchet
    or French bread
salt and pepper, to taste

Herbe Broth with Eggs and Cheese and red wine

In a large mixing bowl, mix together the parsley, cheese, sage, and saffron with a potato masher until a thick paste is formed. In a separate pot, bring the pea stock to a boil. Mix in the wine and ginger and simmer on medium-low for 25 to 30 minutes, stirring occasionally. Mash the peas with a potato masher until a thick mush is formed. Soak the bread in the stock and set aside on a plate. Stir the eggs whole, not scrambled, into the broth and continue to simmer on low until poached.

Using a slotted spoon, place the poached eggs on the bread, sprinkle with salt and pepper, add a dash of ginger, and serve hot. Garnish with orange slices or herbs for color. Serves 2 to 4.

Mortis de Chicken (Chicken Pate on Toast)
French/English recipe, ca. fifteenth Century

Here is an authentic hors d'oeuvre that once enticed many a court in ancient France and throughout the English Isles. This smooth-tasting pate known, also as a mortis, is delightful as an appetizer or simple snack to accompany warm bread or crackers, baked brie, and fresh fruit. Serve on a large platter, bedded with kale or fruit to add color and flair, and offer a selection of sauces, such as Comosta, a sweet vinaigrette, liver sauce, or simple ground sauces like garlic and leek to add diverse flavors.

Mortis de Chicken and a Claret wine

Ingredients
2 large chickens (cut up and diced small)
5 tablespoons heavy cream
1½ cups unsalted almonds, ground
5 to 10 tablespoons rosewater (optional)
4 tablespoons raw or natural sugar
2½ tablespoons salt
2 to 4 tablespoons ground multi-colored
    peppercorns

Boil the chickens in salted water. When fully cooked, remove from the water and let cool. Remove all the meat and discard the bones and skin. (Though early cooks might have crushed the bones along with the mixture, we will only use the meat.) If you like, you can return the bones to the water and simmer for several hours to make stock for future recipes.

Cut the cooked and cooled chicken meat into small pieces and grind with a hand-held blender, or place in a food processor until the meat becomes a thick paste. If you like, add the rosewater, ground almonds, and sugar, and blend until the pate is rich and smooth. You may thin the pate with a little chicken stock or 2 tablespoons of extra virgin olive oil. Add the salt and freshly ground pepper and mix well. Spread generously on toasted bread cut in fancy triangles and squares and serve with fruit. Serves 8 to 12.

Crone's Four Bean Burgoo

English/Mediterranean recipe, ca. seventeenth century

This recipe was discovered among the personal effects of an indentured slave family that once lived near the ruins of the ancient Turnbull Fort in New Smyrna Beach, Florida. This area was once a planned community to be overseen by Andrew Turnbull, a Scottish physician in the English settlements of the eighteenth century; he and a group of Minorcans worked to secure an outpost for England. The fort and its colony failed, and the slaves were released, but many fascinating things were left behind, recipes among them. This recipe is much older than the fort and its people, however, and would have been enjoyed by Englanders at least 200 years earlier. Using dried beans, herbs, and spices brought over by ships to the new world from the old country, whether from Italy, Greece, or elsewhere in the Mediterranean, this hearty four-bean burgoo stew will satisfy even the most ravenous.

Crone's Four Bean Burgoo and fresh bread

Ingredients
2 cups broad beans
2 cups fava beans
1 cup haricot beans
1 cup white beans
½ pound pork or bacon back (diced small)
1 cup water
1 cup goat's milk
1 cup verjuice or white wine vinegar
10 garlic bulbs (peeled and diced in slivers)
1 cup green onions (peeled and diced)

Place the dried beans in separate bowls and cover with cold, salted water. Let this sit for at least 8 to 12 hours to soften the beans and release unnecessary starches, known as drawing out the gasses. There are many ways of doing this, but this seems to be a time-honored method and makes for soft, flavorful beans. Drain the beans. Fry the pork or finely diced bacon until dark brown. Place all the ingredients in a large bowl and mix well. For the best results, use a crockpot set to low heat, cooking at least 8 hours for a proper consistency. Stir often, making sure the bean mixture is a thick, lumpy mush. When almost ready to serve, turn the heat to high and let cook for at least another hour before serving. If you don't have a crock pot, bake the mixture in a 200-degree F, oven for 4 hours. Serve in deep wooden bowls or on trencher meal bread. Serves 4 to 8.

Elizabethan Pease Pottage (Thick Pea Soup)

ENGLISH RECIPE, CA. SIXTEENTH CENTURY

I prepare this favorite recipe year-round. Basically a thick split pea soup, this pottage was once enjoyed by Elizabethans, both peasants and royals, and will delight even the pickiest diner. I discovered this recipe while attending an Elizabethan festival in Palm Beach, Florida, many years ago. I had the chance to sample this wonderful soup during the banquet, and to be fair, it tastes much better than it looks, but then again, many of the foods of centuries past did not always look as delightful as they tasted. This recipe is reputed to be of English origin, finding its way to America's colonial period. This dish is certain to inspire you, and will please vegans too.

Elizabethan Pease Pottage with Manchet and herb cheese

Ingredients
4 cups water
4 cups pure vegetable stock
8 cups early peas
8 cups sweet peas
1 sweet onion, diced small
4 large cans spinach
2 cups heavy cream
5 to 8 tablespoons olive oil
5 tablespoons coarsely ground pepper
1 cup freshly made croutons

This soup was traditionally made with fresh peas; however, canned peas are just as good here. If using peas and spinach from a can, include the liquid. In an extra large pot add the water, vegetable stock, peas, diced onion, and spinach. Bring to a rolling boil, stirring continuously. Reduce heat to medium-low and simmer 2 to 4 hours. Once the mixture is soft, mash it with a potato masher or hand-held blender. Unlike many such pottages, which are thick and mush-like, this broth is thin and easily sopped up with bread.

Return to a boil for several minutes, stirring constantly. Reduce heat and let simmer for another hour or more. When ready to serve, add a little heavy cream to each serving bowl and stir in, making a swirl effect. Serve with a bowl of freshly baked croutons or long shards of toasted bread for a topping. You may have your spice and herb bowls handy for your guests for added flavor. Serves 8 to 10.

Devonshire Fish Soup
ENGLISH RECIPE, CA. FIFTEENTH CENTURY

I enjoyed this a soup some years back while touring southern England, and found that my hosts could trace this family recipe back to the time of the Hundred Years War. This would have been a local favorite on the English coast, as it is an easy dish to prepare and hearty enough to serve as a meal. Various types of fish were probably used in ancient England, including sea bream, porgy, meagre, croaker, halibut, and mullet. The latter appears to have been the primary fish used. This wonderful soup makes an excellent meal or well-balanced starter.

Devonshire Fish Soup with Trencher bread, green onions and a sharp cheese

Ingredients
5 cups fish or vegetable stock
1 bottle dry white wine
1 lemon, pulped
2 white onions, finely chopped
1 carrot, finely chopped
4 stalks celery, finely chopped
2 leeks, finely chopped
2 to 4 bay leaves (optional)
1 teaspoon ground nutmeg
1 teaspoon cayenne pepper, powdered
½ teaspoon cloves, powdered
1 medium fillet of gray or red mullet fillet
1 medium or large fillet of sole
1 large fillet of whiting
24 oysters, in shells
24 shrimp, peeled (optional)
24 crayfish tails, in shells
20 to 25 field mushrooms (any variety)

In an extra-large pot, combine the fish or vegetable stock, white wine, lemon pulp, onions, carrots, celery, leeks and spices, and bring to a rolling boil. Reduce heat to medium-low and simmer for 1 to 2 hours. Scallop the fish into bite-sized chunks and sauté. Slice the mushrooms (unless using button mushrooms, which you will leave whole) and add to the broth, along with the oysters, shrimp, and crayfish. Bring to a boil for a few minutes, and then simmer on low for another 2 to 3 hours. Discard any oysters that do not open, and remove the bay leaves.

When ready to serve, pour the piping hot soup into a large serving bowl or tureen and offer with fresh bread, such as manchet or diar bread and soft butter. Serves 8 to 14.

Bosham Lobster Soup

English recipe, ca. fourteenth century

Paganus folk of the English coasts would have
known the value of the sea and the delightful
bounty it offered. During many fishing runs
in the ancient lands of Bosham, in West Sussex,
or off the coast of Durdle Dor, in Dorset, the
people would have made great effort to meet
their seasonal seafood supply. Nothing could
compare to fresh lobster, and this wonderful
shellfish would have been served a variety of
ways. This simple recipe may have been a
precursor of the refined bisque soups we know
today. This soup is best served with dry white
wine and warm manchet bread; it also makes
a fabulous starter for any seafood meal.

Bosham Lobster Soup with artisan carrots and lemons

Ingredients
2 large fresh lobsters, cooked
5 tablespoons butter
1 medium red or white onion, chopped fine
3 stalks celery, chopped fine
1 cup carrots, cooked and chopped fine
1 can clam juice or oyster juice
6 tablespoons olive oil
1 cup dry vermouth or dry white wine,
    divided
2 large cans stewed tomatoes
1 whole bay leaf (optional)
3 to 5 garlic cloves, peeled and mashed
½ teaspoon cayenne
½ teaspoon fennel seeds, crushed fine
1 cup heavy cream
salt and pepper, to taste
5 to 10 shards of toasted manchet bread

Shell the lobster, cut into tiny morsels, and set aside, saving the shells. In a small saucepan,
melt the butter and stir in the finely chopped vegetables, cooking slowly on medium-high heat
for 6 to 10 minutes, without browning. In a large pot, combine the clam or oyster juice, olive
oil, and half of the vermouth or white wine, and heat to medium-high. Add the lobster shells,
discarding the feelers and head, and cook 5 to 10 minutes. Reduce heat to low, add the salt
and pepper, and turn occasionally. Pour in the stewed tomatoes with their juice; add the bay
leaf, garlic, cayenne, and sautéed vegetables. Cover and simmer for 30 to 35 minutes.

Remove the shells and bay leaf and puree the mixture. Return it to the pot and add the lobster
meat, season with any remaining spices to taste, and gently simmer for another 25 to 40 minutes,
stirring occasionally. For the lobster cream, pour the remaining vermouth or white wine into a
clean saucepan. Heat to medium-high and slowly mix in the heavy cream, stirring occasionally.
Simmer on low until ready to serve. Ladle the soup into bowls or deep plates, and then swirl the
vermouth cream sauce from the middle outward. Serve with toasted bread shards and soft butter.
Serves 4 to 6.

Cawl Cymreig (Welsh Stew)

WELSH RECIPE, CA. SIXTEENTH CENTURY

Cawl cymreig (pronounced cowl) is a national dish in Wales, but it has been served in regions of England for centuries. Every Welsh household has its own recipe, with variations in seasonal roots, herbs, and vegetables, but most will agree that Cawl is an all-time favorite. Though the meats used in ancient times would have included lamb, pig, or beef, or a mixture of these meats, along with fresh winter vegetables such as turnips, leeks, potatoes, and cabbage, the addition of Scottish Swede turnips, or French-turnips, otherwise known as *navets*, are also common today.

The late Welsh chef-extraordinaire Kenneth Thorne would have suggested that traditional Cawl be eaten with hand-made wooden Cawl-spoons, which were designed to keep one's mouth from burning on the piping hot stew.

Traditional Cawl with field potatoes, Stilton cheese and Cock Ale

Moreover, he would also have insisted that a good piece of Welsh cheese and hot bread would have been the proper thing to serve with it. I would suggest a traditional farmhouse cheese called Caerphilly. This mild, crumbly white cheese from South Wales spreads nicely on warm bread.

Ingredients
2 tablespoons lard or bacon fat
2 onions, coarsely chopped
2 parsnips, roughly chopped
4 carrots, sliced in chunks
1 Swede turnip, coarsely chopped
1 pound brisket of beef, in small cubes
1½ pounds lamb, in small cubes
1 gallon of beef or lamb stock
1½ pounds smoked bacon (collar or shoulder)
13 whole black peppercorns
½ teaspoon clove powder
1 bay leaf
1 sprig of fresh thyme
1 pound white or new potatoes, diced small
8 leeks, thinly sliced, divided

In a large iron skillet, heat the lard or bacon fat until slightly browned. Add the onions, parsnips, carrots, and turnip, and cook until soft and brown. Remove with a slotted spoon and set aside. Add the meat to the pan and brown until fully cooked. Return the vegetables to the meat, add the bacon and herbs, and continue browning. In a large pot, bring the stock to a rolling boil and add the meat and vegetable mixture with its oils. Cover and bring to a boil, then simmer for 2 to 3 hours, stirring occasionally. In the last 30 minutes of cooking time, add the diced potatoes and half the leeks. Dole out into wooden bowls and garnish with the uncooked leeks. Serve with cheese and bread. Serves 4 to 6.

Blaunche Porre (Chicken, Leek, and Onion Mush)

ENGLISH/FRENCH RECIPE, CA. FIFTEENTH CENTURY

This dish originated in England but appears in various forms in French kitchens, too. The English would have used sweet spices, such as nutmeg and cinnamon, where the French may have added more creams and cheeses and pungent herbs like sage or tarragon. This "mush" is essentially a chicken and onion stew, but because of the unique spice mixture, it has been served as a morning dish as well. Indeed, dishes like this one work for all occasions and at all hours. The spice mixture, known as powder douce, has been used in practically every English dish from medieval times to the present day. You may find this a pleasant change from everyday condiments.

Powder douce is generally made with ground cinnamon, nutmeg, ginger, and sugar, and sometimes other spices in varying proportions. It has also been used with ground sea salt, pepper, sage, and cumin, so the mixture may be varied to complement any dish.

Blaunche Porre

Ingredients
2 bunches of white leeks, minced
2 large Vidalia or white onions, minced
5 to 8 garlic cloves, minced
3 cups chicken stock
1 large chicken or capon
6 strands saffron or 1 tablespoon paprika (for coloring)

Powder douce:
1 tablespoon ground cinnamon
1 tablespoon ground ginger
1 tablespoon ground nutmeg
2 to 4 tablespoons natural sugar
salt and pepper (optional)

Mince the leeks, onions, and garlic, and set aside. In a deep pot, bring the chicken broth to a rolling boil and reduce the heat to medium-low. Cut the chicken into long strips, add them to the hot broth, and cook until the meat is white, scooping away any froth that forms on the top. Place the chicken on a cutting board and dice the meat as small as you can. Return to the pot and cook on low heat for 35 minutes, stirring occasionally.

Add the minced vegetables and powder douce mixture and stir. Using a hand-held blender or food processor, puree the mixture until it is thick and chunky. (This is an excellent dish to serve to the elderly or those who have trouble chewing, as it is nutrient-rich.)

Add the saffron or paprika. This can be served alongside another meat dish, like venison, beef, or mutton, or simply with a side of warm bread or bread stuffing. Serves 4 to 6.

Coastal Crab Cakes
ENGLISH/FRENCH RECIPE, CA. SIXTEENTH CENTURY

This crab cake recipe would have been popular in Elizabethan-era courts and on the French coasts—in the ancient Catalan fishing village of Collioure and throughout the Nord-Pas de Calais region of France. The traditional recipe called for piment d'anglet, or French Basque fryer peppers, which would have been a new delicacy for the English, brought over as gifts from Spanish nobility in the fifteenth century. One thing is certain: the English made an art of the crab cake.

Ingredients
1½ pounds crabmeat, shredded
1 medium red bell pepper, seeded and minced
1 small green bell pepper, seeded and minced
4 shallots, divided
2 garlic cloves, minced
1 stalk of celery, minced
1½ teaspoons fresh or dried dill, minced
4 tablespoons fresh parsley, minced
½ cup plain bread crumbs
dash cayenne pepper
1 teaspoon coarsely ground, multi-colored pepper
2 large eggs, beaten
6 tablespoons olive oil, plus more for frying
3 large tomatoes, diced

Cheese sauce:
½ pound English Cheshire cheese
½ cup goat's milk (whole cow's milk works too)
½ cup white wine (any dry chardonnay is good)
1 tablespoon coarsely ground peppercorn

Place the crabmeat in a large bowl, picking through it to remove any shells. Mix in the minced peppers, half of the shallots, garlic, celery, dill, and parsley. Mix in the plain bread crumbs, cayenne, and ground pepper with the egg until moist. Form the crab mixture into 6 patties and wrap each in wax paper, then refrigerate for 30 minutes. In a separate bowl, mix the minced tomato and remaining shallots with the 6 tablespoons olive oil. Set aside.

Coat a large skillet with olive oil and fry the crabcakes on high heat until each side is nicely browned and crisp. If you prefer, you can bake the cakes on a cookie sheet at 350 degrees F. for 20 minutes or until brown.

To make the sauce, place the Cheshire cheese, goat's milk, wine, and pepper in a medium-size saucepan, and slowly melt on low heat until thick. When it begins to bubble, reduce the heat to warm and set aside until ready to serve. Offer in separate bowls or in one serving bowl, and garnish with dried herbs such as tarragon or parsley. Offer these delectable cakes with the tomato and shallot mixture and warm bread. Serves 2 to 4.

Coastal Crab Cakes and warm Seafarer's Flip

Crème Almaundys (Cream of Almond Soup)

FRENCH RECIPE, CA. SIXTEENTH CENTURY

This delightful bisque was common throughout medieval Spain and France and traveled on to the new world, where it got a great reception. Many traditional households still enjoy this unique aperitif in one form or another, ranging from ground or powdered nuts made into a thick broth and stewed in goat's milk, or as a thin broth made with saffron. This recipe, however, calls for almond milk. If you cannot find almond milk, use regular milk and 1 teaspoon of almond extract.

Offer this unique soup as a starter to any meal consisting of game bird or hen. Crème Almaundys is also a wonderful soup to eat when you're feeling under the weather, as it was believed to have healing qualities.

Crème Almaundys with Diar Seed Bread, cheese and salted almonds

Ingredients
1 cup unsalted blanched almonds
1 medium-size capon or game bird
4 cups almond milk
3 cups water
1 tablespoon ground nutmeg
1 teaspoon ground cinnamon
½ teaspoon allspice
1 teaspoon salt
1 cup heavy cream
1 sprig fresh mint

Crush the almonds into a moist powder and set aside. Put the capon in an extra large pot, add the water, and bring to a boil. When the water begins to overflow, reduce the heat and remove the bird, setting it aside for another recipe. Remove any froth and continue cooking the water on low heat for 20 minutes. Stir in the almond milk, cover, and simmer for 15 to 20 minutes. Add the spices, salt, and pulverized almonds and continue to simmer for one hour. Stir occasionally so the soup does not scald or clump.

Remove from the heat and strain the liquid through a cheesecloth, then pour the strained soup into a serving bowl. In a separate bowl, whip the heavy cream with a whisk until thick and pour it into the almond soup. Stir well, sprinkle on some nutmeg, and garnish with the mint. Serve with chicken or game bird or alone with warm bread and butter. Serves 4 to 8.

Stewed Pompion (Spicy Pumpkin Soup)

ENGLISH RECIPE, CA. SEVENTEENTH CENTURY

If there is one soup that best fits the autumn equinox and the Samhain season in particular, it's this tasty soup. It likely traveled from the New England colonies to the Virginia settlements at Jamestown, Williamsburg, and Roanoke. I have read the middle-English recipes several times, and the best translations state that this stew was cooked over a small fire all day so that the pumpkin meat was a dark brown and thick, so that it would "furnish the meat of the sea with goodly favor," meaning that this is a sweet side dish that works well with bitter or salty meals. Try pompion stew before or with any of the fish dishes in this book. For something both ancient and delightful, try it as a dessert, served with heavy cream and sprinkled with nutmeg.

Stewed Pompion with Ginger Wine

Ingredients
4 cups pumpkin or squash meat
6 tablespoons whole butter
4 tablespoon raw or natural sugar
2 teaspoons ground ginger
2 teaspoons ground nutmeg
4 teaspoons apple cider vinegar
8 to 10 fresh mint leaves, washed
salt and pepper, to taste

Cut the pumpkin or squash meat into bite-size pieces and wash well, making sure there are no seeds. Fill a large, deep pot or crockpot halfway with water. Add the diced pumpkin or squash, half of the spices portions, and sugar. Set on medium-low and prepare to give this dish a whole day to cook down. Begin this process a day ahead of your scheduled meal or at least in the early morning to make sure the consistency is just right. When the pumpkin meat begins to sink, you'll know it is absorbing the fluids. Add the apple cider vinegar and cover. When the day has passed, you will notice that the squash takes on a dark brown, almost baked apple look.

Preheat oven to 300 degrees F.

Ladle the soup into a deep bowl or casserole dish and dash the other half of the spices over the top. Bake at 300 degrees for 10 minutes, until the top begins to brown. Place the mint leaves around the dish and season to taste. Add more of the ginger if you want a more tart taste, or more sugar for a sweeter taste. Or offer two separate spice bowls to give your guests a choice. Serves 4 to 6.

Chapter 5. Time-Honored Entrées and Robust Delights

BEAST OF WOOD, FISH OF SEA, FOWL OF AIR, DOTH GRACE THY TABLE FAIR

"An intelligently planned feast is like a summing up of the whole world, where each part is represented by its envoys."
—Jean-Antheleme Brillat-Savarin, The Physiology of Taste (1825)

The Feast, by an unknown artist, c. fourteenth century. *Courtesy of Society for Creative Anachronism, Arts and Sciences of the Middle Ages and Renaissance*

ow we come to the wonderful delights of ancient cookery that reflects the very nature of our Paganus ancestors, as seen in the many lexicons and cookbooks of antiquity. These centuries-old recipes still have the power to ensnare memories of the regal feasts and offer a sense of the traditional for modern-day use. The recipes and cooking methods that follow are intended to bring back a sense of our intense histories, which will hopefully find their way to your banquet table with equal flair.

Some time ago, while visiting the Metropolitan Museum of Art in New York City, I found myself intrigued by *Peasants Dancing and Feasting*, by the Flemish artist David Teniers the Younger. This lively oil painting, ca. 1660, depicts happy people dressed in the common garb of the day, dancing and conversing; others sit and drink and eat, the men likely speaking of the crops due to come in or the haul of fish that day. Some women sit with their husbands, some dance, and others feed their babies, all expressing the gaiety of simple pleasures. Like the joyful people of that ancient painting, we should express our pride in ways we know best, through color and light, food and drink, and song and dance!

The foods that follow represent those enjoyed by Paganus peoples dating as far back as the late Roman Empire to the dawn of the eighteenth century. They highlight the foods and libations of the English Isles and Europe, and would have followed the new-world settlers to Salem, Massachusetts, and Jamestown, Virginia. Venison pottage, roast beef and crisps, and stuffed loin of lamb are wonderful examples of ancient foods that will find favor in your home, while the more exotic recipes, such as Chawetty meat tarts, Anglesey eggs, rabbit and onion pye, and Welsh rarebit will astound your guests and make a legend of your culinary skills.

Grete Pye

ENGLISH RECIPE, CA. FOURTEENTH CENTURY

No holiday meal would have been complete without a hot Grete Pye gracing the table. Even the poor might have one on special occasions. Made with meats such as chicken, rabbit, venison, pork, or beef, or several meats mixed together, these tall pies adorned with leaves or other designs were synonymous with medieval supping well into the Tudor age.

Ingredients

For the pastry dough:
1⅔ cups flour
1 stick of unsalted butter, in small chunks
2 tablespoon suet or cooking lard
1 egg, loosely beaten
2 egg whites (beaten thin)

For the filling:
1 pound of boned chicken breast
1 pound wild duck meat
1 pound of pork
⅓ cup dates (softened in water and chopped fine)
⅓ cup currants or raisins (softened in water and chopped fine)
½ cup prunes (softened in water and chopped fine)
1 teaspoon ground cinnamon
½ teaspoon ground cloves
½ teaspoon ground mace
½ cup beef stock
1 tablespoon corn flour
4 hardboiled egg yolks (crumbled)
salt and pepper (to taste)

Preheat oven to 425 degrees F.

Place the meats in a medium-sized pot of salted water and parboil gently for 10 to 15 minutes. When tender but not thoroughly cooked, drain and let cool on a plate. Slice the meat into small chucks and set aside.

Make the pastry: In a large bowl, mix the flour, butter, and suet with your hands until the dough is like thick bread crumbs. Add a little chilled water and continue mixing until blended. If you have a pastry blender, this will save you time. Add the beaten egg and continue to mix, creating a *pâte à foncer*, similar to French pastry dough. Place this on a floured surface and cover with a damp towel. In a separate bowl, combine the meats, softened fruits, and half the spices, and set aside.

Coat a 9-inch pie pan with the beaten egg whites. Line the inside of the pan with the pastry dough, pinching the edges down at the top. Be sure not to break any part of the dough. Place the pie pan in the oven for about 10 minutes or until the dough begins to brown, but don't let it darken too much. Remove and let cool.

In a small sauté pan, heat the beef stock on medium-high until it bubbles slightly and add the corn flour, mixing well until it becomes thick and creamy. Reduce the heat and set aside to cool. Add half the minced meat and fruit mixture and half the spices to the partially baked pie and spread out evenly, then add half the cooled beef stock and the crumbled, hardboiled egg yolks. Repeat the layering with the remaining meat and fruit mixture, spices, stock mixture, and hardboiled egg yolks. Roll out most of the remaining dough and place over the top of the pie pan, pinching the edges evenly. With the last scraps of dough, make little leaves and decorate as you see fit, almost as you would making a dessert pie or wedding cake. Be as elaborate as you wish. Brush the top of the dough with beaten egg yolk, reduce the oven to 325 degrees F., and bake for 35 to 40 minutes.

Present the pastry on a large platter on a bed of greens. Slice and serve like a cake. Offer with clapshot potatoes, hardboiled eggs, and vegetables. Serves 6 to 8.

Grete Pye with Stepony wine, seasonal fruit and cheeses

Caws Wedi Pobi (Welsh Rarebit)

WELSH RECIPE, CA. SIXTEENTH CENTURY

Caws Wedi Pobi, known simply as Welsh rarebit, is a bit like the American grilled cheese sandwich. This recipe was found in the seventeenth-century journal of a lady living in the county of Glamorgan, which is today Cardiff, the nation's capital, though it probably dates back to before Renaissance times. The ingredients called for a kind of cheese that no longer exists in Wales, or in England, for that matter, but any choice, sharp cheddar will do. Processed cheeses will not melt properly, nor offer an authentic taste. If you're going all out, try using genuine Welsh cheddar from the Pembrokeshire Cheese Company (see appendix). This is one of the most faithful brands I have used.

Caws Wedi Pobi was normally served to hunters who came home without any game. But young children will enjoy it, too.

Caws Wedi Pobi with leeks and cheddar

Ingredients
2–3 ounces butter
8 ounces sharp cheddar cheese (coarsely grated)
1 large egg yolk
salt and pepper, to taste
2–3 tablespoons dark beer or ale
4 slices bread (toasted)
5 tablespoons dark mustard (served in a side dish)

In a saucepan, melt the butter over medium heat. Stir in the cheese, egg yolk, salt, and pepper. When the melted cheese begins to bubble, add the dark beer or ale. Reduce the heat to low and toast the bread, which should be cut into thick wedges. Pour the cheese mixture over the toasted bread on each plate. If you wish, offer dark mustard in a separate bowl so your guest can add as much as they like.

Consider variations, such as adding a poached egg on top or a side of boiled potatoes and leeks or other seasonal vegetables. This recipe was enjoyed when times were rough and the winters bitter and cold. Serves 4.

Cavalier's Venison Pottage (Stew of Deer)

Pan-Celtic recipe, ca. seventeenth century

This simple venison stew echoes a time when Irish and English hunters would scour the woods for deer, boar, and fowl. It was popular from the early days when Cavaliers and Roundheads were battling across the English Isles, right on down to the new world settlements. Hunting deer or quail in certain counties could mean imprisonment or death for ancient Paganus peoples. But the risks were worth it when they caught a stag or doe and were able to stave off hunger.

Growing up in Danvers, Massachusetts, I experienced the joy of indulging in this recipe. It dates to the early seventeenth century when my ancestors lived in the high country of Wales. If you are unable to find venison, you can substitute veal or a tender cut of beef. However, I would recommend ordering it online, as the succulent meat is unforgettable and a testament to our ancestors.

Cavalier's Venison Pottage, cheese and Manchet bread, field beans and Raisin Stepony Wine

Ingredients:
8 cups vegetable stock
2 pounds venison (cubed to bite-sized pieces)
4 large white onions
4 parsnips
4 large beets
1 cup claret wine or burgundy
3 tablespoons olive oil
1 bunch sorrel, cut fine or coarse
2 tablespoons ground ginger
2 tablespoons ground nutmeg
2 tablespoons ground mace
2 tablespoons ground cloves
2 tablespoons sea salt
1 to 2 dashes of coarsely ground pepper

In a large, deep pot, bring the vegetable broth to a rolling boil and reduce to medium heat. Cut the meat into bite-sized chunks. In a small frying pan coated with the olive oil, braise the meat on high heat for about 5 minutes on each side. Dice the onions, parsnips, and beets. Combine all the ingredients in the large pot, including the wine and spices, and cover. Reduce heat to low and simmer 4 to 6 hours. Stir occasionally, removing any froth from the top.

I like to prepare this dish the night before a dinner party so that the meat practically melts in your mouth. Serve in deep bowls and offer thick slices of warm manchet bread, and a plate of sharp cheese shards. Serves 6 to 8.

Medieval Capons in Concy
ENGLISH/IRISH RECIPE, CA. THIRTEENTH CENTURY

Capons in Concy, otherwise known as confit, dates to at least the early medieval period and continues to be enjoyed to this day. This dish is best served on individual platters or from a fancy roasting pan, and garnished with roast vegetables, hardboiled eggs, and warm Diar bread with herb butter. Add whole roasted garlic for an authentic medieval dish.

Ingredients:
2 large capon or chicken
2 cup chicken stock (homemade or
   organic is best)
1 stick butter
1½ cup bread crumbs (fresh, torn small)
2 tablespoons powder fort
saffron threads (5 to 6 strands)
12 eggs (hardboiled, crushed or split)
cloves (ground for garnish)
salt and pepper (to taste)

Medieval Capons in Concy with green onions, herb cheese and boiled eggs

Preheat oven to 320 degrees F.

Place the capons in a large roasting pan and rub butter all over each bird. Roast for 25 to 30 minutes, or until the bird is half done. Set aside to cool. Boil the eggs until firm and let cool. When the capon is cool to the touch, strip the meat in sections and return it to the pan, arranging in a flower-like shape. Discard the bones. Pour the chicken stock over the meat and cook over medium-high heat until the stock begins to perk. Reduce the heat to low and simmer for 30 minutes, or until the meat is cooked through.

Remove from the pan and place on a serving platter. Using a strainer, pour the chicken stock into a clean pan and add the finely torn bread crumbs. Bring this to a simmer and stir until thick. Add the powder fort, the remaining butter, and the saffron and continue to stir. Arrange the meat in a flower formation on a large platter, or in a fancy roasting pan. Take 6 of the hardboiled eggs and separate the yolks from the whites. Sprinkle the crumbled egg whites over the meat, covering every piece. Remove the bread sauce from the heat and pour over the meat and egg whites, blanketing everything. Arrange the egg yolks to top and dust with ground clove. Scatter the remaining hardboiled eggs around the pan or platter. Serves 6 to 8.

Romano-Anglo Roast of Lamb
ENGLISH RECIPE, CA. FOURTEENTH CENTURY

Here's a rare favorite from France and the English Isles, though it dates back to around the fourth century when the Romans discovered a new and tasty condiment. Made with ground mustard seed and verjuice or a young wine called "must," a flavorful creation was born. The thick paste was used for anything from food to medicine, and it was popular throughout Europe by the thirteenth century. Many types of mustards, called mostarde, were being reinvented with spices, fruits, vinegars, and seeds. But it was the mustard that appeared in Dijon, France, that found the greatest favor. Though this lamb dish is certainly delicious served plain, the ancients would have added these spicy mustards along with the slightly pungent flavor of rosemary to create a tantalizing essence for bitter or bland meats. This dish is best served with Scotch clapshot potatoes or frumenty, field peas, and warm bread with a side of herbal butter sauce or garlic sauce for dipping.

Romano-Anglo Roast of Lamb with Rosemary Potatoes, boiled mushrooms and Cock Ale

Ingredients:
3 to 3½ pounds lamb shoulder
1½ cups Dijon mustard
⅓ cup verjuice or dry white wine
2 tablespoons mustard powder
8–12 sprigs of fresh rosemary

Preheat oven to 425 degrees F.

Wash the meat well, removing any bone spurs. Let it sit in a pan of salted water for 15 to 20 minutes to remove any clotted blood and absorb the salt. Arrange on a baking pan with the meat pieces touching each other. In a medium-size bowl, mix the mustard, verjuice or dry wine, and mustard powder into a thick paste. This adds a wonderful flavor and will reduce the lamb's pungency. Spread the mustard mixture over the meat evenly. Strip the rosemary leaves from the stem and spread the leaves over the meat.

Place the pan in the oven and roast for 20 to 25 minutes, then reduce the heat to 300 degrees F. and continue to roast until the meat is tender, allowing about 15 minutes for every pound. Baste with any leftover mustard mix to keep it from getting too dark. If necessary, loosely cover the pan with tinfoil. Place on a large platter with roast rosemary potatoes and warm manchet bread, and offer with a dark ale or a chilled glass of Metheglin ginger wine. Serves 6.

Stuffed Loin of Pig

WELSH RECIPE, CA. SIXTEENTH CENTURY

This traditional pork recipe has been a Jenkins family favorite for more than a century, gracing my grandmother's banquet table since childhood. Originating from the Glamorgan region of Wales, my great-grandparents had brought many of their time-honored customs to America, including cooking techniques. They survived off the land with common vegetables like turnips and leeks, and by catching game and fish.

Some families had their own pigsty if they lived in the country. This allowed them to enjoy pork throughout the year, barter with their neighbors, and even pay their taxes with pork when currency was sparse. This dish is generally reserved for special occasions and holidays, and is served with bouquet garni sauce and hearty stuffing.

Ingredients
3 to 4 pounds boned pork loin or butt
1 quart water
5 tablespoons salt (for making the stock)
1 bunch bouquet garni
½ cup flour (plain or seasoned)
5 tablespoons bread crumbs
2 feet of cooking string, to bind the meat

Stuffing:
2 small onions, finely chopped
4 tablespoons lard or meat drippings
1 cup bread crumbs
1 tablespoon orange zest
1 tablespoon parsley, chopped fine
1 tablespoon chives, chopped fine
½ tablespoon dried mint leaf, chopped fine
salt and pepper, to taste
2 tablespoons orange juice
2 tablespoons orange juice
2 jumbo egg, beaten and divided
1 cup Pembrokeshire cheese (grated coarsely)
2 tablespoons salted butter

Sauce:
½ pint meat or vegetable stock
1 medium onion, sliced
1 tablespoon flour
½ cup currants or goose berries (optional)
1 dash salt and pepper

Bouquet garni:
3 sprigs thyme, fresh
3 sprigs savory, fresh
2 large bay leaves
5 springs fresh parsley
5 inches of cooking string

Preheat oven to 400 degrees F.

If the pork was purchased rolled and tied, remove the string and unroll the meat. Make a long slit along one side of the meat so that it opens and lays out flat. Put the water and salt in a large pot and bring to a slow boil. Add the bouquet garni, reduce the heat and simmer for 30 to 40 minutes. Allow the stock to cool for at least 30 minutes.

Prepare the stuffing. In a medium-size saucepan, cook the onions and lard until just soft. Stir in the bread crumbs, orange zest, parsley, chives, mint, and salt and pepper. Stir in the orange juice and half the beaten eggs to bind the mixture to a medium thickness. When this mixture cools a bit, add the grated Pembrokeshire cheese and butter, turning until well mixed. Using a spoon, spread half of the stuffing inside the meat evenly, and then roll up the meat firmly. Tie with the cooking string and set aside.

Spread the flour on a plate, and the remainder of the stuffing mixture on another plate. Roll the meat in the flour, brush with the remaining beaten egg, and roll in the stuffing mixture. Place the meat in a roasting pan, cover, and bake for 1½ hours or until medium-dark brown. Baste often with the sauce mixture.

To make the sauce, strain the vegetable stock or any leftover juices from the pan. In a separate frying pan, fry the sliced onion in a little fat from the roasting pan until it is softened and browned. Stir in the flour and add the stock and berries. Bring to a boil for no more than 2 minutes. Continue to stir or whisk rapidly, remove from the heat, and set aside. When the meat is done, place on a serving platter. Carve the meat into ½-inch slices. Place each slice on a plate and spoon on the sauce. Offer this tasty dish with traditional frumenty stuffing or clapshot potatoes and a fresh herb salad. Add warm diar bread and cold ale or dark beer, or a red wine. Serves 4 to 6.

Stuffed Loin of Pig, bouquet garni and apples

Roasted Honey Chicken
ENGLISH RECIPE, CA. FIFTEENTH CENTURY

This time-honored recipe dates to the high medieval period, when feasting tables were so grand that they were arranged only once a year by the lord and lady, or when a major victory was secured for a kingdom. At times, the foods were so elaborate that such a banquet would equal the most lavish ceremonies imaginable. In contrast, however, the simple man and woman would have to get by with what they could manage, and chickens were a primary food to eat and to barter with, so an average home would usually have various birds as a stable diet. This recipe is designed for chickens or capons, but it also works well with turkey, Cornish hens, pheasant, duck, and pigeons. Honey was a major staple

Roasted Honey Chicken, with potatoes, fruits, breads and assorted cheeses

throughout ancient history, used in everything from wines and brews to roasting sauces for meats and fish. Although raisins are used here, colonists new to America would have used indigenous berries and nuts. Feel free to use cranberries, raspberries, gooseberries, and even mulberries.

Ingredients:
1 whole chicken, washed and dried
¼ cup sea salt
1 apple, sliced
1 tablespoon butter
1 cup kale, for bedding

Glaze per chicken:
⅓ cup clover or wild flower honey
½ cup apple cider vinegar
½ cup dry white wine
½ cup extra virgin olive oil
 ½ cup dried raisins (white and dark are best for color)
1 tablespoon dried sage
1 tablespoon dried mint
1 pinch of ground cloves

Preheat over to 325 degrees F.
Wash and dry the bird and rub with the butter and salt. Stuff the chicken with the apple slices and place in a roasting pan. Place in the oven and roast for about 45 minutes, or until the meat is cooked but not dry.
 In a saucepan combine the honey, vinegar, wine, olive oil, and raisins and cook on medium-high heat until the mixture begins to bubble and caramelize. Reduce the heat to low and simmer, stirring occasionally. When the chicken is done, remove it from the oven and spoon the glaze over it. Return it to the oven to allow the glaze to melt and saturate the meat, then remove. Place on a platter bedded with kale and add more of the glaze if desired. Sprinkle the chicken with sage, mint, and cloves, and serve with warm bread, steamed vegetables, and a parsley and sage salad. Serves 1 to 2 per chicken.

Aberdeenshire Pheasant
SCOTCH/ENGLISH RECIPE, CA. EIGHTEENTH CENTURY

Introduced to Europe and England along the Asian Trade Routes, the pheasant quickly became a delicacy. By the seventeenth century, the more than fifty breeds of pheasant were almost hunted to extinction in the west, making the bird popular with the rich and powerful, while pigeon hunting among the lower classes was prohibited. On occasion, though, average folk would be treated to this delicacy when stray pheasants wandered into their community. In Scotland, especially throughout the northern sections, such as in Aberdeen, hunting season begins in fall with a traditional flair. This recipe was discovered in an Aberdeenshire family cookbook dated 1702. It would have been braised or baked to a golden brown and served with oatcakes or bannock bread, with sides of Swede turnips and potatoes, which were called neeps and tatties.

Today, we can purchase these tasty birds online or in specialty stores and Asian markets for a modest price. The best pheasants are Himalayan Monal and White Eared, which in

Aberdeenshire Pheasant with mushrooms and Ginger Wine

the United Kingdom can run from upward of £240, to the Cabot's Tragopan pheasant, which can cost as much as £800, or close to $1,300 for two birds—certainly, a meal fit for royalty. Regardless, this is a simple and relatively low-fat game bird that will find favor with even the most refined guests.

Ingredients
2 ringneck pheasants (Note: hens weigh 2–3 pounds, cocks weigh 3–4 pounds. One
    full-grown bird should serve two people.)
⅓ cup olive oil
4 cloves garlic per bird (sliced thin or crushed)
1 pound thickly cut smoked bacon
dash of oregano
sea salt and coarsely ground peppercorns

Preheat oven to 300 degrees F.
Clean each bird thoroughly, removing most of the skin, except for the top of the breast and the legs. Cover each bird with olive oil and salt and pepper. Using a large iron skillet or an individual, seasoned skillet, place the garlic cloves on the bottom, and then each bird on top of that, arranging the bird so that it is completely inside the pan. Arrange the bacon around the breast of each bird, tuck the ends inside the skillet. Sprinkle the birds with salt and pepper, and place the skillets in the oven for 30 to 40 minutes. If the juices start to overflow the pan, ladle out the excess and discard. When the skin turns golden and crispy, reduce heat to about 150 degrees and bake another 10 minutes. Serve in the mini-skillet on a heat-tolerate surface. Sprinkle the oregano over bird, and serve with Scotch clapshot potatoes, field greens, or an herb salad, along with warm bread and cheese. Serves 4 to 6.

Rissoles (Meat Patties or Stuffing)

FRENCH RECIPE, CA. SIXTEENTH CENTURY

Here's a dish with as many styles and appearances as there are French cheeses. It can be made as a meat-filled pastry or formed into patties like a hamburger, and served with sweet apple compotes or mashed potatoes. It can serve as a meal or an hors d'oeuvre. Some historians believe this French recipe dates to the sixteenth century dish, while others believe it is much older, more likely medieval in origin. In spite of its vague history, rissole meat pies, tarts or patties are filling and uniquely tasty, and will honor any table nicely. Serve with a fresh apple or berry compote, with a side of Dijon mustard as a sauce and a sprinkle of dried lavender, and with steamed vegetables.

Ingredients
½ pound beef or veal (if using beef, carne picada style is best)
½ pound wild boar or pork, minced
5 large hardboiled eggs, crushed
2 cups bread crumbs, ground medium-fine
2 jumbo eggs
4 large leeks, small dice
5–8 springs fresh sage, minced
½ pound Cardamom, Bleu d'Auvergne, Contrôlée, or any blue cheese, crumbled to
    medium-sized chunks
1 teaspoon salt
½ cup olive oil
½ cup water
3 tablespoons olive oil
3–5 tablespoons dried French lavender

Apple compote:
2 large apples, diced into small chunks
⅓ cup sultanas or black currants (optional)
1 cup water
5 tablespoons wildflower honey
1 or 2 dashes powdered cardamom

Combine the apple compote ingredients in a deep pot and heat on medium-high until the mixture starts to bubble. Reduce the heat to low and simmer, stirring constantly. You'll want the compote to be thick and chunky, having absorbed the fluids. While the compote is cooking, mince the meats and mix in a large bowl with the bread crumbs, hard-boiled eggs, leeks, olive oil, and powder fort to form a thick, chunky paste. Add the raw eggs, leeks, spices ,and cheese, and mix until thoroughly combined. Form the mixture into 4-inch patties and set aside. Sprinkle the salt and finely minced sage on a dry plate, patting the mixture onto each meat patty.

In a deep pan, combine the olive oil and water and place on medium-low heat until the liquid begins to pop. Gently add each patty to the pan and cook until it turns gray. Turn over and sprinkle any remaining sage and salt over all. Spoon the apple compote on each plate or serve in a separate bowl. Before serving the rissoles, turn the heat to high for a few moments to make sure the meat is thoroughly cooked. Pierce each one with a fork to be sure the inside is done. Remove with a slotted spoon, sprinkle with the lavender, and offer with clapshot potatoes, steamed vegetables, and warm bread for a tasty treat of old France. Serves 4 to 6.

Rissoles with apple compote and garlic

Newtown Rabbit and Onion Pye

WELSH/IRISH RECIPE, CA. FOURTEENTH CENTURY

This traditional Welsh recipe is likely much older than the fourteenth century, as it can be found in several books of Welsh, Cornish, and Irish chronology. Onions and other edible roots continue to grow freely in the countryside, and freshly caught rabbit is always delicious, although you can substitute duck, chicken, pork, or beef if you desire.

Ingredients
For the pastry:
2 cups white flour
½ cup wheat flour
2 eggs
1 teaspoon salt
½ cup oil or lard
½ cup water

Filling:
1 large rabbit (at least 1½ pounds of boned rabbit, or 1 medium duck or 2 chicken breasts skinned and diced small)
2 ounces lard or other cooking fat
3 medium-sized onions, chopped fine
2-3 large carrots, cut in long chunks
10 slices smoked bacon, thickly sliced and diced
1 sprig thyme, minced
1 bay leaf (optional)
1 pint chicken or vegetable stock
salt and pepper, to taste

Rinse the meat, dry, and set aside. In a large saucepan, melt the lard or other fat over medium-heat. Add the onions, carrots, bacon, thyme, and bay leaf and cook for 15 to 20 minutes, or until the vegetables are soft. Add the rabbit and braise for another 10 to 15 minutes, leaving the meat a little red. Remove the meat and set aside. Add the stock, salt, and pepper to the liquid; cover and let simmer on low heat for about 1 hour. Remove from the oven and let cool. Discard the bay leaf.

Preheat oven to 300 degrees F.

To make the pie crust, mix the white and wheat flour, eggs, salt, oil, and water in a bowl, and form the dough into a ball. Add more water or flour if necessary and let sit for an hour or two. Roll out most of the dough (leave some of a top crust), place in an earthen, deep-dish pie pan, and salt and pepper liberally. Bake until slightly risen and golden, then remove from the oven and let cool. Fill the pie dish with the cold rabbit mixture and cover with the remaining dough, pinching the edges and pressing down firmly. Make a vent to let the steam escape, and use the pastry trimmings to cut out decorative leaves or other ornaments for the top. Brush the pastry with egg yolk and bake for 60 to 70 minutes, or until the crust is a golden-brown. Let cool slightly. Serve with rapas sive napes, clapshot potatoes, and freshly steamed vegetables. Serves 4.

Newtown Rabbit and Onion Pye with smoked cheese and assorted olives

Anglesey Eggs

WELSH/IRISH RECIPE, CA. FIFTEENTH CENTURY

This recipe was likely enjoyed when the Vikings used the island of Anglesey as an outpost, and possibly as far back as the Roman age when Anglesey and all of England was occupied, when the first trade routes crossed the Menai Strait and the Irish Sea. Anglesey Eggs is a simple dish, but one that farmer and noble would have enjoyed equally.

Anglesey Eggs with boiled eggs, Manchet bread and cheese

Ingredients
8 to 10 eggs, hardboiled
3 to 6 large leeks, chopped
1 pound mashed potatoes
5 ounces sharp cheddar cheese, grated thick
½ stick salted butter
1 tablespoon plain flour
½ pint milk, at room temperature
½ teaspoon ground nutmeg
salt and pepper, to taste

Preheat oven to 350 degrees F.

A tasty way to use up leftover potatoes and cheese, this recipe is still enjoyed in southern England. Make mashed potatoes in the typical fashion, or use the Scotch Clapshot recipe, which combines turnips or rutabagas for an interesting, historically accurate flavor. Boil the eggs, peel, and let cool. Boil the diced leeks for 5 to 10 minutes, until slightly soft. Strain out the water and mix with the hot mashed potatoes. Beat in half of the butter until the mixture is fluffy. Spoon this into a greased, ovenproof dish and set aside.

In a separate saucepan, melt half of the butter and stir in the flour. Cook for about 3 minutes, whisking constantly. Remove the pan from the heat and vigorously whisk in the warm milk. When smooth, return to the heat and bring to a boil, then simmer gently until a thick mush is formed. Add the nutmeg, most of the grated cheese, and salt and pepper to taste. Halve the hard-boiled eggs and lay them face-up on the bed of leeks and potatoes, then cover with the remaining cheese sauce, followed by the rest of the grated cheese. Bake until bubbly. Serve sprinkled with dried herbs, such as thyme, parsley, or oregano, and warm bread. Add several slices of full-bodied, peppered bacon for a truly authentic Welsh-Irish dish. Serves 4 to 6.

Cornish Sausages
CORNISH RECIPE, CA. SIXTEENTH CENTURY

This sausage dish is one of my favorites, though a rare treat, as making sausage from scratch is time-consuming. In ancient times, most middle-class families owned a pig or two. The use of herbs and spices distinguishes different cultures as much as any one food or libation, and this thyme-infused recipe echoes the Cornish people.

Sausage-making is not as hard as you might think. For variations on this recipe, purchase casings from your local butcher or simply hand-form the meat mixture into links, flour well, and fry.

Ingredients
4 cups boiled ham or ground veal
4 cups lean, charcuterie-style pork, ground
2 tablespoons dried thyme, minced
1 tablespoon sea salt
3 large eggs, beaten
4 cups bread crumbs (ground fine)
½ cup white flour
½ cup extra virgin olive oil or lard
2 tablespoons ground peppercorn

Cornish Sausages with green onions, grilled mushrooms, garlic, and Cock Ale

In a large mixing bowl, combine the minced ham or veal and pork, thyme, sea salt, and beaten eggs, and mix into a thick mush. Add the bread crumbs and continue mixing until the mixture is bound and pliable. Cover the bowl with wax paper and refrigerate for at least 30 minutes. Use your hands to form the meat mixture into average-sized sausages. Set them on the plate of flour and coat well. Place an oiled skillet on medium-low heat and fry in the oil until browned. Serve hot. If using pre-made skins, stuff and tie off the ends with cooking string. After browning the sausages, discard the strings and sear the ends. Serve with eggs or the Cornish Bacon and Egg Pye. Serves 5 to 8.

Cornish Bacon and Egg Pye

CORNISH RECIPE, CA. FIFTEENTH CENTURY

This dish will serve supper as nicely as it will breakfast. Many of our ancestors' meals were suitable for any time of the day; eggs were not just for the morning meal. Most common-folk breakfasts consisted of fruit, bread, and cheese, though meat was often on the menu, too. This dish's origins are hard to place. Some date it to the Britons in the Dark Ages. It was probably a variation of the popular German egg kuchen and later the French quiche, open-faced pies containing every meat, vegetable, or fruit imaginable. Serve hot or cold and offer it with a Parsley, Onion and Sage Salade, or a Folk Herbe Salet and English biskets.

Bacon and Egg Pye with seasonal fruit

Ingredients
For the pastry:
2 cups flour
2 eggs
½ cup vegetable oil
½ cup water
1 teaspoon salt
1 egg yolk

For the filling:
6 rashers of bacon, cut into pieces
2 to 4 sprigs of parsley, chopped fine
5 eggs
¼ pint milk
3 sprigs fresh sage, chopped fine
salt and pepper, to taste

Preheat oven to 400 degrees F.

To make the pie crust, mix the flour, eggs, salt, oil, and water in a bowl until the mixture holds together. Add more water or flour if necessary. Form into a ball, cover with wax paper, and refrigerate overnight.

Roll out the dough as thin as possible on a floured cutting board. You can use a large pie pan or small, individual pie pans. Place the dough into a greased pan, lay the bacon on top, and dust with the parsley. In a separate bowl, beat the eggs and milk and pour over the dough and bacon, then season with sage, salt, and pepper. Cover with the remaining dough and press the edges with a fork. Cut slits on the top to vent steam. Brush with the egg yolk and bake for 40 minutes. Serve with orange wedges, steamed vegetables, and homemade Cornish sausages for an authentic Cornish breakfast. Serves 4 to 6.

Dr. Dee's Roast Beef and Crisps

ENGLISH RECIPE, CA. SIXTEENTH CENTURY

Here is a roast beef dish that will have your guests pleading for more. A delightful meal in any century, this entrée echoes a time of great elegance and sophistication, when Queen Elizabeth's courts were filled with foreign ambassadors and dignitaries, and when the tables were as illustrious as the royals' clothing. This dish is said to have been a favorite of Dr. John Dee, the court's famous sage, astrologer, and ear to the virgin queen herself. Roast beef is still on the menu today, though historically there are many different versions of this time-honored dish.

Roast is typically served with traditional Yorkshire pudding, an eighteenth-century side dish, though history tells us that having a bread-like stuffing, or in this case, a doughy coating, was quite common. This recipe is much like the modern beef Wellington, but instead of being coated in a pâté de foie gras and a flaky pastry shell, it calls for a sweet and spicy batter crust and fruit. When accompanied with traditional frumenty, Welsh creamed leeks, and the newly discovered potato—a fledgling delicacy in sixteenth-century England—and served with a cool and spicy Stepony wine, you and your guests will experience a medley of tastes not enjoyed for at least the last five centuries.

Ingredients
½ cup flour
2 tablespoons dried rosemary
1 tablespoon dried basil, crushed
1½ tablespoons dried thyme, crushed
½ teaspoon sea salt
1 egg yolk
5 pounds beef roast, tied with butcher's string
½ cup flour
10 tablespoons butter
½ cup dried apple rings
1 cup dates, pitted and halved
1 cup figs, halved and stems removed

Batter:
1 cup flour
½ cup whole wheat flour (optional)
2 jumbo eggs
½ cup whole milk (goat's milk is best)
½ teaspoon salt
½ teaspoon baking powder
3 tablespoons brown sugar
½ tablespoon ground cinnamon
1 teaspoon nutmeg
fresh parsley, chopped
basil leaves for garnish

Preheat oven to 350 degrees F.

In a medium-sized bowl, mix together the flour, dried herbs, and sea salt, and set aside. To prepare the beef, beat the egg yolk to a froth and coat the beef with the ½ cup flour.

Using a Dutch oven or cast iron pot with a cover, melt the butter on high heat and sear the beef until brown. Move the meat to a plate and thoroughly coat with the flour-herb mixture, making sure there is a thick coating on the top and sides. Place the roast in a Dutch oven or cast iron pot, cover, and bake for 2½ to 3 hours. Remove from the oven and let cool to the touch.

Raise the oven temperature to 400 degrees F.

To make the batter for the crisps, mix 1 cup flour with the eggs, milk, salt, baking powder, brown sugar, and spices to form a thick batter. Discard the butcher's string on the beef and ladle the juices over it, then place the apples, dates, and figs on top and around the sides and pour on the batter. For a crisper shell, add the whole wheat flour to the batter. Bake, uncovered, for 10 to 20 minutes until the coating is lightly browned. The "crisps" should fall off naturally. Gently transfer to a large platter and spoon remaining juices and fruit around the meat. Sprinkle with parsley and arrange the basil leaves on top. Offer with roasted potatoes and vegetables to re-create an authentic feast of the ancient world. Serves 6 to 8.

Dr. Dee's Roast Beef and Crisps with roasted field Potatoes and artisan Carrots

Chawetty Tarts (Venison or Veal Pies)

ENGLISH RECIPE, CA. FIFTEENTH CENTURY

Chawetty tarts, though as old as the crusades, were a staple food during the reign of the Tudors. They continue to be a favorite for many citizens of England today in one form or another and are related to the popular Christmas treat mincemeat pie. This spicy, semi-sweet meat pie is a true reminder of how ancient England played an important part in the way Europe prepared its food for centuries to come. And, it was only natural for the English settlers to have carried on the tradition to the new world, as Sir Walter Raleigh settled Virginia for Queen Elizabeth I.

This recipe is very much like contemporary meat pie recipes. The difference is in the unique flavors of medieval Europe and the Middle East.

Ingredients
For the pastry:
3 cup all-purpose flour
2 large eggs
1½ teaspoons sea salt
¾ cup unsalted butter
12 tablespoons water
1 large egg yolk, for brushing

For the meat filling:
1½ to 2 pounds venison or veal, in bite-size cubes
1 tablespoon salt
8 tablespoon currants, chopped
5 tablespoon dates, chopped
5 to 8 threads saffron
¾ tablespoon ground ginger
¾ tablespoon of black pepper
½ tablespoon ground mace
¼ tablespoon ground cloves
½ cup beef stock
½ cup red wine (burgundy works best)
½ tablespoon of vinegar
6 egg yolks, some for brushing
salt and pepper, to taste

To make the pie crust, combine the flour, eggs, salt, butter, and water in a bowl until it holds together to form a dough. Add more water to flour if necessary. Cover the dough ball with wax paper and refrigerate for at least 30 minutes. (Or use store-bought roll-out pie dough.)

To prepare the filling, combine the cubed meat, salt, currants, chopped dates, saffron, and spices, and sauté in a light cooking oil. Add the beef stock and wine and simmer until most of the juices have evaporated. Remove from the pan and let cool.

When the dough is ready, dust a clean surface with flour and roll out the dough into two 5-inch circles, saving some for the top crust. Salt and pepper liberally.

Preheat oven to 350 degrees F.

Combine the vinegar and egg yolks with the meat mixture, stirring until blended and thick. Transfer this mixture to the dough, forming a ball of meat at the center. Bring the sides up around the meat to form a bowl. Cover each pie with another piece of dough, crimping at the side to form a round container for the meat filling. Make several small slits or a small hole in the middle of the top layer so that steam and juices can escape. Brush more egg yolk over each pie to create a golden hue when baked. If you like, use any remaining dough to make animal, castle, or flower shapes, and attach them with the beaten yoke. Bake for 45 minutes, and then reduce heat to 325 degrees F. for another 30 minutes until the crust is a light golden-brown. Serve this dish with Scotch clapshot potatoes and steamed vegetables. Serves 4.

Chawetty Tarts with Cock Ale and seasonal fruit

Baked Carp with Spices and Figs
English recipe, ca. sixteenth century

"The Carp is the queen of rivers, a stately, a good, and a very subtle fish that was not at first bred, nor hath been long in England, but is now naturalized."
—*The Compleat Angler* by *Izaak Walton, 1653*

Baked Carp with dates, figs, and fresh fruit

This unique fish dish is made with a medley of spices that will delight as much as it will fascinate. I have added figs, as the Elizabethans considered this food important medicinally when consuming large quantities of food. But beyond that, this recipe has remained a favorite for its taste and texture. This recipe calls for carp, but other fish like tilapia and porgy work well, too, as they have a similar texture to the meat.

Ingredients
1 to 1½ pounds whole carp, porgy, or tilapia
1½ cups figs or prunes, chopped small
1 cup butter
2 tablespoons sea salt, coarsely ground
5 tablespoons olive oil
4 tablespoons chopped basil
5 to 10 kale leaves
1 tablespoon ground cloves, for dusting

Purchase only the freshest carp or similarly textured fish. Clean, scale, and gut the fish, and then place them in a pan of saltwater or brine for several hours or overnight in the refrigerator. This is done to soften the fish and get rid of fishy oils. Prepare the prunes or figs. Dice half of the fruit, making sure to remove any pits or stems. For the figs, try using Turkish figs, which are the most historically accurate. Remove the fish from the water, pat dry with a paper towel, rub the butter around the fish, and apply sea salt liberally. Stuff the fish's gullet with the chopped fruit and some of the butter, creating a mush.

Place the stuffed fish in a large baking dish on its belly and facing upward, as if swimming, and then place the remaining prunes or figs around the fish. Sprinkle on the cloves, cover the fish, and bake at 200 degrees F. for 2 hours. Transfer to a large platter lined with green kale, surrounding the fish with extra prunes or figs, vegetables, and hardboiled eggs. For color, sprinkle with the basil. Offer with frumenty and Cauli Verdi pottage and a dry white wine or Cornish ginger wine. Serves 4 to 6.

English Coffyn Pyes

ENGLISH RECIPE, CA. THIRTEENTH CENTURY

While touring the ancient grounds of Dunwich Village, a coastal parish in Suffolk, England, a few years back, I stopped at a local pub for a bite to eat. I sampled a classic meal known as a Ploughman's Lunch, which consisted of bread, sharp and cream cheeses, pickled onions, and fruit chutney. I was also offered a little tart the owner had made that morning. These wonderful little gems are one of the most time-honored foods of the ancient English Isles and were traced back to before the crusades. The proprietor confided that these coffyn pyes were a family recipe dating to the sixteenth century, and that they were loved by the village people. She was right—these little pyes are tasty, and filling, too. They would serve ancient Paganus folk as a common meal, for these on-the-run pies were literally designed to be carried as an edible lunchbox. Made with seasoned lamb, spices, minced fruit, vegetables, or mushrooms, you'll find this recipe easy to prepare. Serve these little pies alone or with Welsh creamed leeks or fresh steamed vegetables and a variety of cheeses for a hearty meal worthy of any English pub.

Ingredients:
Pastry:
2 ½ cups flour
1 large egg yolk
1 teaspoon sea salt
2 tablespoons vegetable oil
½ cup cold water

Filling:
4 tablespoons olive oil
1 pound fresh lamb, diced small
½ cup red wine
½ cup wild mushrooms, thinly sliced
1 large purple onion, finely chopped
1 cup prunes, pitted and diced small
1 tablespoon ground ginger
2 tablespoons fresh thyme, chopped
½ cup heavy cream
1 cup beef stock
1 large egg yolk
salt and pepper, to taste

Preheat oven to 400 degrees F.
To make the pie shells, mix the flour, egg yolk, salt, oil, and water in a bowl and form into a dough ball. Add more water to flour if necessary. Wrap in plastic and refrigerate overnight. Roll out the dough thinly and cut out 8 5-inch circles or squares.
For the filling, heat the olive oil in a large frying pan, add the diced lamb a little at a time, and brown on medium-high heat. Reduce heat to medium-low and add the wine, mushrooms, onion, fruit, spices, and herbs, cooking until tender. Cover, reduce the heat to low, sauté for 10 minutes.

Turn off heat and stir. When cool, spoon a tablespoon or more on each of piece of dough. Top with another piece of dough, or simply fold over, pasting down the edges with a fork. Place on a baking sheet and make 2 small slits on the top of each pie. Whisk the yolk of 1 egg with the heavy cream and brush over the pies evenly. Add salt and pepper to taste. Bake for 20 to 25 minutes until the pies are golden brown. Serve warm and with cheese and fruit for an authentic ploughman's lunch. Serves 4.

English Coffyn Pyes with garlic, spices, and seasonal berries

Codfish in Gravy
ENGLISH RECIPE, CA. SIXTEENTH CENTURY

As ancient Spanish, French, and English ships sailed the high seas and around the Caribbean Islands, their nets filled with culinary bounty. They found new and tasteful ways to serve the many varieties of fish and sea life. This delectable codfish recipe is light enough to serve as a lunch or as the main meal with hearty sides.

Codfish in Gravy with hardboiled eggs, ripe olives, and Seafarer's Flip

Ingredients
1½ to 3 pounds codfish, scaled and cut in fillets
5 tablespoons white flour
¼ cup butter
1 cup goat's milk or sweetened whole milk
1½ teaspoons dried dill
1 cup dry white wine
¼ cup heavy cream
2 jumbo eggs, hardboiled and mashed
1 teaspoon cinnamon
2 large lemons, wedged or sliced
6 to 12 hardboiled eggs, for platter

Preheat oven to 375 degrees F.

In a large baking dish, soak the codfish fillets in cold water for a few hours or overnight in the refrigerator. Place the fish in a deep sauce pan and slowly heat to a good simmer, trying not to boil. When the fish is cooked through, drain the water and transfer to a medium-deep baking dish. Repeat this process to remove fishy oils and soften the fish. Then return to the baking dish and set aside.

To make the sauce, mix together the flour, butter, and milk in a saucepan and cook on medium-high heat. When it begins to bubble, add the dill and wine and stir until thick, reducing the heat to low. Be sure not to overcook or scald the milk during this process.

When you begin to see a few more bubbles, add the mashed hardboiled eggs and heavy cream and stir. After about 5 minutes, pour the thick sauce over the fish evenly in the baking dish and then sprinkle liberally with the cinnamon. Bake for 35 to 40 minutes. If you want the sauce to brown, reduce the heat to 300 degrees and bake a little longer. To serve, place lemon slices around the baking dish and offer with a Salet of Lemmones, a bowl of Bosham Lobster Soup or Devonshire Fish Soup and traditional English biskets, along with a dry white wine or a warm mug of Seafarer's Flip. Serves 4 to 6.

Chapter 6. Rich Trimmings and Traditional Side Dishes

THAT WHICH LAY BESIDE THE FEAST, NO MORE THE LESS,
IS GREATER STILL, IN TASTE AND ZEST.

"It is easy to halve the potato where there is love." —Old Irish saying

Feast scene from Richard Pynson's 1526 edition of *The Canterbury Tales. Courtesy of Society for Creative Anachronism, Arts and Sciences of the Middle Ages and Renaissance*

No book of recipes, ancient or new, would be complete without a section on side dishes and culinary trimmings. Therefore, I present here several authentic recipes that would have sustained both the Paganus folk and noble from the early medieval period to the High Renaissance. Although many early side dishes were as simple as a loaf of bread, a shard of cheese, and greens from a field, on rare occasions the common family would have the opportunity to feast.

When Sir Walter Raleigh introduced potatoes and tobacco to England in the sixteenth century, the world of eating and social living changed drastically in England. Although Americans had been enjoying the potato for centuries, many Europeans would come to know this vegetable as a cure for famine, and for bland meals, too. Later, as our ancestors traveled to Virginia's Jamestown or the New England colonies of Salem and Popham, right on down to the southern regions, such as the Province of Georgia and La Florida, they discovered many new fruits, vegetables, and spices, thus adding to the old culinary kitchen customs and creating many of the foodstuffs we take for granted today.

It was common for communities and families to have gardens containing a large selection of vegetables and herbs that could be pickled or dried for the winter. In 1525, a wealthy landowner named Thomas Fromond compiled the now famous book on herb lore, *Herbys necessary for a gardyn*, a manual of herbs and vegetables used by cooks, decorators, and physicians. The many culinary foods one should grow included potherbs, pottages of herbs, herbs to distill, herbs for sauces, and ornamental and medicinal herbs. There was basil, borage, and beets; chives, carrots, coriander, and dandelion; dill, fennel, garlic, and leeks; marjoram, mint, and nettle; onions, parsley, and sage, and radishes, spinach, and thyme. The wealthier the family, the more they had growing in their gardens, including orchards of apples, pear, and other exotic fruits that would have been introduced by ambassadors of foreign lands or from conquest.

As history commenced, more vegetables, herbs, and fruits were added to the gardens of common families and villages. Potatoes and melons; gourds from Asia; squash, pumpkins, and peppers from the colonies; and new grains would now feed the masses. Simple dishes like Scotch Clapshot, one of the Europe's first potato dishes, and Frumenty, a fulfilling wheat stuffing, were favorites among our ancestors. Other side dishes like boiled turnips, called rapas sive napes; carrots and parsnips, known as carotea et pastinacas; and a stewed cabbage known as cauli verdi would have graced the tables. These new recipes became as important as the main meals among court nobility and commoner alike.

The following dishes will serve any occasion with a singular ease and delight. And, although some of these ancient recipes may at first appear difficult to prepare, keep in mind that our ancestors, who survived on practically nothing, created these delicacies that have lasted for centuries. When served with an ample selection of breads and salads, pottages, soups, and hors d'oeuvres, you'll notice that your modest table will take on the appearance of the feasting halls of our ancestors.

Scotch Clapshot Potatoes (Mashed Potatoes)

SCOTTISH RECIPE, CA. SEVENTEENTH CENTURY

It should not be surprising that one of America's favorite dishes, mashed potatoes, is not an original North American dish. Potatoes traveled long and far, from places like Peru and the Andes Mountains, to finally grow in the fertile regions of Europe and the English Isles. Although many other countries would have enjoyed imported potatoes from time to time, the potato was considered a lower-class food. By the late seventeenth century, however, it would be the Scottish and Irish who inspired this recipe known as clapshot, a favorite of sailor, soldier, and commoner. Serve with butter and sweet spices to recreate an authentic historical dish.

Scotch Clapshot

Ingredients
10 large potatoes, peeled and sliced
5 large rutabagas, peeled and sliced
3 large turnips, peeled and sliced
2 to 4 radishes, thinly sliced
1 bunch chives, finely chopped
½ cup butter
1 teaspoon ground nutmeg (optional)
salt and pepper, to taste

Peel the potatoes, rutabagas and turnips, slicing them into medium-size chunks. Thinly slice the radishes. Place the vegetables in an extra-large pot of water and boil for 30 to 40 minutes on medium-high heat, stirring occasionally. Transfer to a large bowl, add the chives, and mash with a potato masher. The mashed potatoes should be thick and lumpy, the English way. For the butter sauce, melt the butter slowly in a saucepan and add the nutmeg. Salt and pepper to taste and pour over the potatoes or offer hot in a gravy boat. Serves 6 to 8.

Cauli Verdi (Cabbage Pottage)

SPANISH RECIPE, CA. FIFTEENTH CENTURY

This simple, yet interesting, side dish comes from a fifteenth-century manuscript found in the Biblioteca Universitaria de Granada in Spain. The manuscript, along with woodcuts and colorful illustrations, shows just how important this vegetable was in ancient times. Offered as a side dish, cauli verdi would have been prepared for large banquets, for humble family meals, and even as a main course. The added greens and cheese make this dish filling, nutritious, and uniquely tasty. With the assistance of translators, I was able to reproduce this fascinating side dish in its traditional form.

Cauli Verdi with green onions, olives, and Manchet Bread

Ingredients
3 tablespoons extra virgin olive oil
½ head green or purple cabbage, shredded
½ bulb of fennel, thinly sliced
15 Brussels sprouts, cored and cut in thin slices
5 tablespoons fresh lemon or orange juice, divided
1 apple, shredded
½ cup Manchego, Parmesan, or Romano cheese, coarsely grated
sea salt and pepper, to taste
1 cup toasted walnuts, crushed or halved

Preheat oven to 400 degrees F.

In a large skillet, heat the olive oil over medium-high heat. Add the shredded cabbage, sliced fennel bulb, and Brussels sprouts, and mix well. Add half the lemon juice and saute for 5 to 10 minutes, and then remove from heat. Add the shredded apple and the other half of the lemon juice and mix until everything is soft. Spread the contents into a deep baking dish, top with cheese, and bake for 15 minutes. To serve, place the walnuts around the edges or add them to individual servings in earthen bowls.

You may add a few poached eggs on top to create an interesting medieval breakfast, a common practice when food was scarce. Serve with any meat or fish dish and warm bread. Serves 4 to 6.

Roast Potatoes and Rosemary
German recipe, ca. eighteenth century

It's hard to imagine that our ancient ancestors did not enjoy the simple pleasure of eating a potato until the tail end of the Age of Enlightenment. Europeans had to wait for the Spaniards to return from their South American raids to be introduced to these wondrous gems, and it wasn't until the 1740s that King William of Germany began cultivating the potato in his country. The potato of old would not have been the gigantic Idaho spud we're accustomed to today. Many people enjoyed smaller, colorful varieties of potato, such as the French yellow and Peruvian purple fingerling potatoes and baby Dutch potatoes. Add these to common varieties to create a colorful and tasty side dish.

Roast Rosemary Potatoes with Gouda cheese and Cock Ale

Ingredients
1 bag Bamberg potatoes (about 12)
2 bags baby Dutch potatoes (yellow variety)
2 bags fingerling potatoes (multi-colored variety)
1½ cup olive oil
salt and pepper, to taste
10 to 15 sprigs of rosemary
1 bag of kale, for garnish
dash of truffle salt (optional)

Preheat oven to 250 degrees F.

Fill a large pot halfway with water and bring to a boil. Add the potatoes and cook on medium-low heat for about 25 minutes, stirring occasionally, just until soft. Do not overcook. When a knife can pierce the flesh with ease, the potato is ready. Remove the potatoes with a slotted spoon and place them in a large metal baking or roasting pan. You may need two or three pans. Let the potatoes cool to the touch, carve a small X on one side of each potato, and pour the oil over them. Turn each potato so that it is covered in oil. Dash some salt and pepper over the potatoes and bake for 25 minutes. Remove the pan from the oven, and carefully turn each over potato with metal tongs, making sure the potatoes are coated with oil.

Place the potatoes on a large serving platter on a bed of kale or other greens. Garnish with rosemary leaves. If you like, offer with samples of flavored butters, a small bowl of salt for sprinkling, and if you can afford it, some authentic truffle salt, which can be purchased at specialty gourmet stores, or from online sources. The flavor is truly fantastic. Serves 8 to 12.

Frumenty (Medieval Wheat Stuffing)

ENGLISH RECIPE, CA. FOURTEENTH CENTURY

If there is one traditional dish in the history of medieval cooking, it is the world's first example of a grain stuffing known as frumenty. Frumenty was served as a main dish for the common family, but nobles loved it, too, as a side dish. Paganus folk throughout England and Europe often ate it as a way of focusing on a good harvest in the coming year, and as food for celebrating solstices and holidays. It is also a dish for vegans, when not prepared with meat or its juices, though traditional frumenty is best served as a side with game birds and heavy meats such as venison, boar, or mutton. Because it's such a filling dish, you may enjoy it alone or with other hearty vegetables, such as Welsh creamed leeks or rapas sive napes.

Traditional Frumenty with cheddar and chilled Chardonnay

Ingredients

3 cups pearl barley or bulgur wheat
3 cups water
3 beef boullion cubes (if serving with venison or beef)
5 jumbo egg yolks, beaten
2 strands saffron or ½ teaspoon paprika
1 cup almond milk or cow's milk
1 cup raisins or mulberries (if making a breakfast dish)
½ cup heavy cream (if making a breakfast dish)
5 tablespoons butter

Preheat oven to 300 degrees F.

The grains to make frumenty may be purchased from your neighborhood health food store or gourmet grocer. Though pearl barley is best, you can also use bulgur wheat. Simply add the barley or wheat to boiling water for several minutes, stirring continuously. Reduce heat to medium-low and continue to stir. After about 10 minutes, reduce the heat to low and cover. Add the beef boullion cubes and drippings from the meat and continue cooking for another 25 to 30 minutes until the kernels burst open and soften. Stir occasionally, as the mixture becomes as thick as oatmeal.

Add the egg yolks and saffron or paprika and let simmer for 10 to 15 minutes. Add the butter and almond milk or cow's milk with a little sugar and a tablespoon of almond extract. Turn all until well-mixed, and then scoop the stuffing or breakfast dish into a medium-sized baking pan or casserole dish and bake for 20 to 25 minutes.

This hearty recipe is excellent for stuffing pork and game birds or mashed to make a thick English-style pudding served with beef dishes. Add raisins or ripe mulberries along with a little brown sugar for a sweet breakfast. Any way you wish to serve it, frumenty will become a favorite. Serves 4 to 6.

Welsh Creamed Leeks

WELSH RECIPE, CA. SIXTEENTH CENTURY

This is one Welsh recipe that will grow on you. Thought to have been a favorite food of Welsh farmers as far back as the seventh century, the leek root was also worn on military clothing to identify Welsh soldiers from the Saxon troops. Leeks soon became a primary source of nourishment when times were difficult, forming the basis for many different meals. Creamed leeks were traditionally eaten with roast mutton or beef, and the typical Welsh ploughman's lunch might consist of creamed leeks with cheese, bread or biskets, and perhaps some meat, if available. Creamed leeks would also serve as a hot pottage for a late night meal.

This recipe will serve as an excellent side dish or as a stand-alone meal.

Welsh Creamed Leeks with Trencher meal bread and herb cheese

Ingredients
Recipe per two servings:
3 tablespoons unsalted butter
4 leeks, thinly sliced
8 shallots, chopped small
5 sprigs thyme
1 pint dry white wine
10 tablespoons double cream
½ cup Pembrokeshire cheddar cheese (or any good-quality extra-sharp cheddar cheese), coarsely grated
salt and pepper, to taste

Preheat oven to 250 degrees F. In a medium-sized saucepan, melt the butter and gently fry the leeks, shallots, and thyme until softened. This should take about 5 to 10 minutes. Next, pour in the white wine and leave to sauté for 5 minutes. Add the double cream and simmer gently for another 5 minutes. (Remember, if you're making for more people; add the appropriate ingredients to make enough for all). Once this is fully cooked, transfer to a baking dish, sprinkle the grated cheese over all, and bake for 25 to 30 minutes. When done, remove and serve hot. You may serve with a side of sour cream, sprinkled with chopped chives to add an extra flair to the presentation, or with cheese and warm bread to create an authentic Welsh treat. Serves 1 to 2.

Carotea et Pastinacas (Carrots and Parsnips)

FRENCH/ENGLISH RECIPE, CA. SIXTEENTH CENTURY

Carotae et Pastinacas is a tasty medley of lightly fried carrots and parsnips sautéed in a rich red wine sauce.

Ingredients
8 to 10 large carrots
5 to 8 large parsnips
1 cup merlot or burgundy wine
½ cup water
5 tablespoons butter
2 teaspoons ground cumin
4 tablespoons red wine vinegar
6 tablespoons olive oil
4 sprigs fresh parsley
salt and pepper, to taste

Carotea et Pastinacas

Peel and slice the carrots and parsnips on the diagonal or use a ribbed culinary tool, such as a julienne peeler. In a medium-sized saucepan, combine the wine, water, and butter and braise on medium heat, just below the boiling point, and then reduce heat to medium-low.

Add the vegetables and cumin and simmer for several minutes. Add the red wine vinegar, cover, and simmer for 30 to 40 minutes. Transfer the vegetables to a deep serving platter, boil the wine mixture and olive oil, and add more cumin and salt and pepper to taste. Pour the mixture over the vegetables and garnish with parsley. Add a little more butter for a richer flavor. Serves 4 to 6.

Onions in Cumin Sauce

ENGLISH RECIPE, CA. FOURTEENTH CENTURY

This dish kept many ancient folk from starving to death during the harsh winter months. Simple to make and suitable as a side dish for pungent meats and fishes or as full meal, this recipe will please vegetarians and others in search of a bold taste and a hearty texture. Whereas some versions of this recipe add wheat bread crumbs to form a thick casserole dish, this rendition offers a lighter taste and a little zing that accompanies other dishes nicely.

Onions in Cumin Sauce

Ingredients
4 cups pearl onions
2½ cups almond milk
3 tablespoons white flour
1 to 2 teaspoons powdered cumin
6 tablespoons clover or flower honey
1 teaspoon sea salt
4 to 5 strands saffron
1 cup apple cider
2½ tablespoons dried tarragon

Preheat oven to 175 to 200 degrees F.
In a large saucepan, combine all the ingredients except the apple cider and tarragon and bring to a boil. When the onions begin to brown, add the apple cider and stir as the steam rises. Reduce heat to low, cover, and simmer until the onions are easily pierced with a fork and the sauce begins to caramelize. Transfer the mixture to individual earthen baking dishes and bake for 1 to 1½ hours. Turn the onions with a spoon and sprinkle tarragon on top. Serve with trencher meal bread. Serves 4 to 6.

Rapas Sive Napes (Boiled Turnips)

ENGLISH RECIPE, CA. FOURTEENTH CENTURY

Rapas sive napes turnips, also called navews, originated in the fifth century and remained popular through the High Renaissance. This is one of the tastiest versions. Rue and sage were believed to have healing properties. It appears that this dish was a health food of the ancient world.

Rapas sive Napes

Ingredients
15 to 20 turnips
1 cup sweet white wine
1 cup chicken or vegetable stock
2 tablespoons extra virgin olive oil
3 tablespoons verjuice or white vinegar
½ teaspoon ground rue or sage
½ teaspoon ground cumin
salt and pepper, to taste
4 tablespoons whole butter

Partially peel the turnips and slice thick, then place them in a bowl of ice water for several hours. In a deep saucepan, combine the wine, stock, and olive oil, and cook on medium-low heat for 15 minutes, stirring occasionally to make sure it does not boil. Cover and reduce the heat to low.

In a deep pot half filled with water, cook the turnips on medium-high heat for 40 minutes or until fork-tender.

Add the wine and oil mixture and boil for 5 to 10 minutes. Remove the turnips and squeeze in cheesecloth to get all the water out, or simply drain until dry. Place the turnips in a large bowl, and add the verjuice (pressed unripe grapes) or white vinegar. If you wish, mash the turnips with a potato masher. Add the herbs, salt, and pepper, and serve with warmed butter. Serves 4 to 6.

Epinards à la Crème (Spinach Soufflé)

FRENCH RECIPE, CA. FIFTEENTH CENTURY

This dish has seen many incarnations over the years. Sometimes it is made with heavy cream, other times with spices and vegetables. In medieval Europe it was known as worte and was composed of leafy vegetables such as cauliflower and spinach, and cream and cheeses. The French enjoyed this dish long before it reached other lands; the British ate it raw until they discovered the culinary wisdom of the French. The spinach was often kept in vats of brine to soften, preserve, and add flavor. This dish may be one of history's first soufflés.

Ingredients
22 ounces canned spinach
4 bags frozen spinach
1 cup green onions, minced
2 cups grated sharp cheddar cheese, divided
2 jumbo eggs
1 cup heavy cream
1 bag fresh spinach
1 cup bread crumbs (plain or seasoned)
2 tablespoons fresh thyme
salt and pepper, to taste

Preheat oven to 300 degrees F.

Drain the canned spinach and place in a large mixing bowl. (If using fresh leaves in place of canned, soak them in brine until soft). Add the bagged frozen spinach, minced green onions, half of the cheese, the eggs, and heavy cream, and stir until smooth. Line the bottom and sides of a lasagna pan with the fresh spinach. Spread the spinach mixture evenly on top. Sprinkle with the remainder of the cheese, and cover the cheese with the dried bread crumbs and thyme. Bake for 40 to 60 minutes until the bread crumbs are golden. Offer in deep bowls, from the baking dish, or with toasted bread and cream cheese as an hors d'oeuvre. Serves 6 to 8.

Epinards à la Crème

Chapter 7. Enchanted Sweets and Pastries

WHEN THE ENDING IS AS GREAT AS THE BEGINNING, WE MUST REJOICE ALOUD.

"Dost thou think because thou art virtuous there shall be no more cakes and ale?"
—William Shakespeare

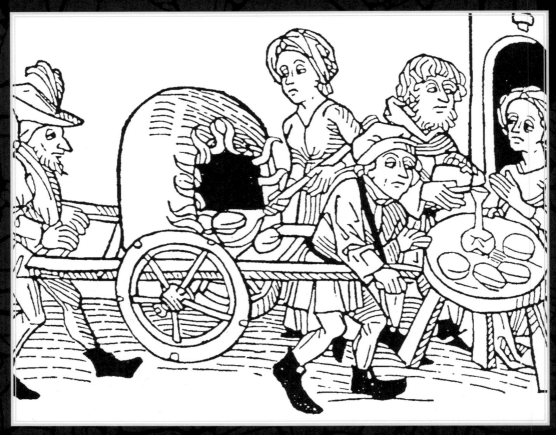

Bread and pye baker, by unknown artist, ca. fifteenth century. *Courtesy of Society for Creative Anachronism, Arts and Sciences of the Middle Ages and Renaissance*

ractically every period of history has had its share of sweets to complete a feast. A common feast would have a selection of fancy desserts that could inspire awe, from exotic fruit compotes and dainty sweet breads and cakes, to sweet meat pies, torts, and marzipan treats that resembled castles, kingdoms, and magical beasts.

The word dessert was first used during the medieval period, and the art of dessert-making developed as a result of cultures intermingling. As England, France, and Spain were expanding their interests across the seas, envoys and ambassadors would bring dessert samples back with them. Though for the most part desserts were quite fantastic, consumed mostly by the nobility, the less fortunate could enjoy a sweet ending to a meal, too. For the Paganus folk of this period and beyond, sweet breads covered with natural sugars and honey were common, as was an egg and almond- milk-soaked pastry known as a darioles. Another typical dessert was fried dough pastries filled with compotes and jellies, an ancient form of doughnut. Almost anyone could enjoy a tantalizing dessert of some sort, while most European and English desserts could be quite extravagant and delightful. When they set off for the tropical islands and the colonies of the new world, they brought with them their traditional recipes, adapting them only slightly with locally available fruits and spices.

With the addition of Native Indian recipes, which have existed in one form or another from Plymouth Rock to La Florida for hundreds of years, and with the many cultural influences, such as from the French Huguenots and the Mediterranean Minorcan settlers, it is safe to say that there is no one correct way to view the cooking methods of our ancient ancestors. Truly, variety is the spice of life.

The recipes that follow were popular throughout medieval Europe, which gives us a clue about the traditional importance of this part of the meal. Dessert has been and remains as important as the feast itself. Whether dining with your significant other or a crowd of friends, it should serve as the final embrace from host to guest.

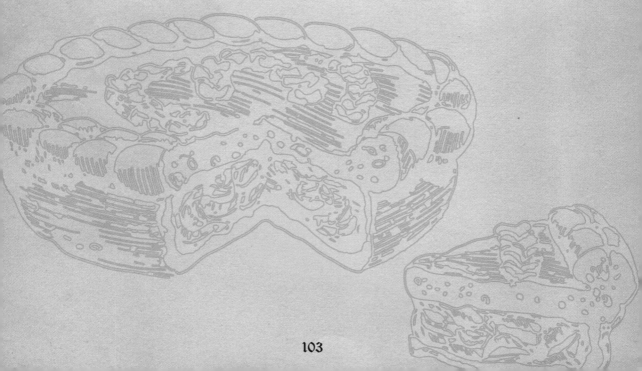

Spicebrede
ENGLISH RECIPE, CA. SIXTEENTH CENTURY

This time-honored gingerbread recipe dates back to at least the thirteenth century, when huge feasts roared in the massive stone halls of ancient castles. Indeed, this sweet dish had graced the tables of England's high courts from the Tudor age to the banquet tables of Queen Elizabeth I and beyond, so it stands to reason that this tasty dessert would sail from colony to colony in the new world.

Ingredients
1 cup clover honey
1 teaspoon powdered ginger
½ teaspoon cinnamon
½ teaspoon ground cloves
⅛ teaspoon ground anise
2½ cups plain bread crumbs
15 to 20 roasted chestnuts (whole or halved)
1 cup seasonal berries (optional for those who cannot eat nuts)

Frosting:
½ cup heavy cream
¼ cup confectioner's sugar
5 tablespoons castor sugar
1 teaspoon white pepper, finely ground
3 to 5 tablespoons brandy
1 tablespoon ground anise seed
1 tablespoon ground ginger, for dusting

Spice Bread with Raisin Stepony Wine and seasonal fruit

In a double-boiler, heat the honey on medium heat for 5 to 10 minutes, making sure it does not scald. When the honey begins to bubble, add the ginger, cinnamon, cloves, and anise, and mix well. Reduce the heat to medium-low and stir. Fold in the bread crumbs and mix thoroughly. Cover and continue cooking over low heat for 15 to 20 minutes. Let cool slightly, and then transfer the contents to a large rectangular bread pan, greased with cooking lard or lined with wax paper.

For the frosting, whip the heavy cream, add the sugars, white pepper, and brandy, and continue to whip until a thick froth forms. Apply the frosting to the cool cake evenly, letting it drip over the sides. Sprinkle with powdered anise seed and powdered ginger if desired. Cover and refrigerate for an hour or two. When ready to serve, place the bread on a bed of warm chestnuts or serve with seasonal berries. Offer Raisin Stepony Wine or a berry cordial. Servings vary.

Medieval Apple and Pear Fritters

ENGLISH RECIPE, CA. FOURTEENTH CENTURY

This recipe has seen many incarnations. The ancient Celts cooked the fruit as a vegetable to accompany mutton or used it to make a fermented wine called Perry. Pear dishes of all sorts were favored in courts and noble halls. Eleanor of Provence, wife of Henry III, maintained extensive pear orchards. Even Eleanor of Castille, wife of Edward I, had pear orchards that produced varieties such as Caillou, Regula, and Pesse-Pucelle for the royal house. Other pear varieties such as Dreyes, Sorells, Gold-Knopes, and Chyrfall were cherished by commoner and noble alike.

In addition to the tasty pear, the apple stands as the most beloved fruit in all of history. When added to the pear in this robust medley, the desire for this fritter becomes clear. Almost any pear variety will work. This recipe can be seen in Tudor-era menus and is best served with a brandy or cognac.

Medieval Apple and Pear Fritters and Cornish Ginger Mead

Ingredients
½ pint ale or beer
1 tablespoon dry yeast
1 large egg
½ teaspoon of sea salt
1 cup plain flour
3 large red apples
3 large, hard pears
½ to 1 cup peanut or sunflower oil
½ cup powder douce

In a large saucepan, heat the ale or beer until warm. Pour about a quarter of liquid into a mixing bowl and add the yeast, whisking when it is dissolved. Add the eggs, salt, and flour and continue to whisk until smooth. Cover and set aside at room temperature for about an hour. Meanwhile, peel and core the apples and pears, and then cut into bite-size chunks. In a deep frying pan or fryer, heat the oil. To test it, drop a little of the batter into the oil. If it pops, turns golden brown, and returns to the surface quickly, it's ready. Using a slotted spoon, dip the apples and pears into the batter mixture until every part is covered, and then carefully dip the battered-fruit into the oil. Turn the fritters over as they begin to brown. When golden-brown, remove and place on a platter lined with paper towels. Serve warm on plates accompanied with the powder douce. For a special dessert, add French vanilla ice cream or serve with a fruit-based after-dinner drink, such as apricot brandy or ginger mead. Serves 4 to 6.

Figgie Hobbin and Clotted Cream
CORNISH RECIPE, CA. FIFTEENTH CENTURY

Figgie hobbin, also known as figgy o'bbin or figgy pudding, has possible connections to other savory holiday puddings like fygeye, crustades, or figge, which is a thick potage of mashed figs, raisins, and bread, crowned with a custard and dotted with sippets. It remains a favorite in many homes throughout the English Isles and is a simple pastry made sweet with lots of raisins or other tiny berries like currants or minced gooseberries. Such fruits are referred to as figs in Cornwall, though you may certainly use figs or dates as a substitute if you like. As popular as spotted dick, another beloved English dessert, figgie hobbin is a singularly staple sweet in Cornwall and is absolutely decadent when served with traditional Cornish or Devonshire clotted cream.

Figgie Hobbin and Clotted Cream with Raisin Stepony Wine

Ingredients
For the pastry:
2 tablespoon lard or vegetable or meat suet
2 cups all purpose flour
1 teaspoon baking powder
1½ cups raisins, currants and/or figs, diced small
5 to 8 tablespoons cold milk
4 tablespoons brown sugar (extra fine is best)

For the clotted cream:
2 cups heavy cream

Preheat oven to 125 to 200 degrees F.

In a medium-sized bowl, rub the lard or beef suet into the flour and baking powder. Mix in the raisins or other fruit, and blend until the dough is stiff. After letting sit for about 20 minutes, roll the dough out on a floured board and form into half-balls about 5 inches in diameter. Make a small cut for ventilation across the top. Brush milk on each piece of dough and sprinkle with brown sugar. Bake for 25 to 30 minutes or until lightly brown. Let cool slightly before topping with the cream.

It's important to make the clotted cream a day or so earlier in order to maintain the proper consistency for this Cornish recipe. In a double boiler, or *bain marie*, cook the cream on medium-heat until it is reduced by about half and has the consistency of butter. When a golden crust forms on the top, transfer it to another bowl. Cover and let stand for about 2 hours. Once cool, refrigerate overnight. When ready to use, whisk the golden-colored crust until it becomes a smooth cream. Dole out the clotted cream at the center of the pastry and garnish with raisins or fruit. Serve warm with tea or other hot beverage. Serves 4.

Iumbolls
ENGLISH RECIPE, CA. FOURTEENTH CENTURY

"Take a pound & a halfe of fine flowre & a pound of fine sugar, both searced & dried in an oven, 6 youlks, & 3 whites of eggs, 6 spoonfulls of sweet cream & as much rose water, fresh butter ye quantety of an egg." — Martha Washington's *Booke of Cookery*, ca. 1755

This ancient cookbook lets the reader know just how simple jumbles are to make, and just how favorable they were in her day. Likely one of the oldest sweets, this simple cookie has been known as jambals, jumballs, and gemmels, and traveled to the colonies of Plymouth, Jamestown, and even the ill-fated Roanoke colony, eventually finding its way into Martha Washington's recipe book. With unique flavorings such as rosewater, coriander, lemon-peel, and aniseed, these cookies were known to last for many months during extended travels.

Jumbles with a sweet Claret wine

Ingredients
3 cups flour
2 cups castor sugar (or any extra fine sugar)
½ cup butter
¼ cup whole milk or heavy cream
3 eggs
3 teaspoons aniseed (or extract)
nuts or candied cherries
½ cup powdered sugar, for dusting
1 tablespoon cinnamon, for dusting

In a large mixing bowl, combine the flour, sugar, butter, milk, and eggs and mix into a thick paste. Adding more or less of the flour or milk until the dough is slightly sticky to the touch. Add the aniseed and mix again until thoroughly blended. Place the dough ball on a sheet of wax paper, roll up, and refrigerate overnight.

Preheat the oven to 350 degrees F.

Flour a cutting board and your hands and form some of the dough into flattened balls. Form pieces into squares and add nuts or fruit on top, such as candied cherries. Another variation is to make walnut-size balls and roll the dough into ½-inch logs, tying them like pretzels or twisting them a few times. You can make any design you wish. You may wish to roll some pieces in powdered sugar or add a dollop of jam. If you want a sturdier cookie like those made for seafarers and soldiers, use whole wheat flour, which will make them more filling.

Place the cookies on a lightly-floured baking sheet and bake for 15 to 19 minutes, or until lightly browned. When cool, dust the cookies with the powdered sugar and cinnamon mixture, or frost with a mixture of 1 cup powdered sugar and ¼ cup milk. Makes about 7 dozen cookies.

English-Style French Toast

ENGLISH RECIPE, CA. SEVENTEENTH CENTURY

Popular in Elizabethan times, this recipe graced noble breakfast tables and café parlors throughout Europe and the British Isles. Though this recipe is translated from the Middle English, having no exact measurements or cooking temperatures, I have experimented enough to make a successful dish. Serve this recipe as a dessert with fresh fruit and ice cream or as a breakfast dish with eggs and meat.

English-Style French Toast with seasonal fruit

Ingredients
1 loaf of French or manchet bread
6 egg yolks
6 tablespoons butter
½ cup raw sugar or extra-fine brown
   sugar
1 tablespoon ground nutmeg
1 teaspoon sea salt

Cut a fresh loaf of French bread into quarter-inch-thick slices. Whisk the egg yolks until light and frothy. In a large frying pan, melt some of the butter and sprinkle the sea salt evenly on top. (Use 1 tablespoon of butter for about every three slices of bread). When the butter begins to pop, dip each slice of bread in the beaten yolks, making sure each slice is well coated. Fry until golden brown, lightly sprinkling the sugar and nutmeg on top while the bread is in the pan. Serve hot with powder douce or powder fort offered in small pinching bowls. Maple syrup was not used before the late seventeenth century, but you may offer a whipped, melted butter with a little sugar mixed in, and fresh seasonal fruit for color and flair. Serves 6 to 12.

Almond Ryce (Almond Rice Pudding)

ENGLISH RECIPE, CA. EIGHTEENTH CENTURY

This particular recipe dates to the late Tudor period. Following the English occupation of North America, it found its way to back to England by the eighteenth century. Consider using unbleached, whole-grain rice for a hearty, oatmeal-like pudding.

Almond Ryce with fresh blackberries and salted almonds

Ingredients
1 cup uncooked white or brown rice
½ cup clove or flower blossom honey
½ cup raw or natural sugar
1 tablespoon salt
1 cup almond milk
1 cup seasonal berries (optional)

There are two methods you can use to cook the rice. One is to cook the rice the conventional way, making sure each grain is fluffy. The second is to soak the rice in cold water before cooking it to get the starch out. Repeat until the water runs clear. This will make for a sticky, clumpy rice with a heavier texture. In a large pot, combine the rice, almond milk, honey, and sugar. Cover and simmer for 20 to 25 minutes. Serve in large bowls with warm almond milk on the side, along with fresh berries or seasonal fruits, and powdered spices. Serves 4 to 6.

Saint Dwynwen's Day Monmouth Pudding
WELSH RECIPE, CA. SIXTEENTH CENTURY

This recipe is named for Saint Dwynwen, a patron saint for lovers that represents the Welsh equivalent of St. Valentine's Day. The tragic story of the fair maiden Dwynwen and her lover, Maelon Dafodrill, was told centuries before Shakespeare penned *Romeo and Juliette*. The recipe, also known as Pwdin Mynwy, echoes the age of King Arthur, when the old and new religions began to meld.

Books and recipes discovered in the ruins of a convent on Ynys Llanddwyn, a remote location off the coast of northern Wales, revealed that Pwdin Mynwy was a common dessert enjoyed during the Roman age. The rich history of this unique pudding can be traced back to around 465 AD and remains a favorite dish for Saint Dwynwen celebrations today. There are several variations of this recipe; this is one of the more faithful and tasty.

Ingredients
For the pudding:
1½ cups raspberries
½ cup brandy
6 ounces plain bread crumbs, finely ground
1 cup, 7 ounces whole milk
2 tablespoons butter
zest of 1 lemon
¼ cup natural sugar
2 tablespoons cocoa powder
3 egg yolks
½ cup raspberry or blackberry jam

Meringue topping:
3 egg whites
¼ teaspoon cream of tartar
½ teaspoon vanilla extract
4 tablespoons caster sugar

In a bowl, combine half the diced berries and the brandy and refrigerate overnight.

Preheat oven to 300 degrees F. Spread the bread crumbs on the bottom of a casserole dish, large glass pie plate, or ramekins and set aside. In a medium-size saucepan, combine the brandied berries, milk, butter, lemon zest, sugar, and cocoa powder, and bring to a light boil, stirring constantly. Pour the contents over the bread crumbs and let stand for 20 minutes. When cool, stir in the egg yolks and bake for 30 minutes or until firm. Remove and let cool. Spread a medium-thin layer of warm jam on top and top with the remaining berries.

For the meringue topping, combine the egg whites, cream of tartar, and vanilla, and whisk until soft peaks form. Add the sugar gradually and whisk until stiff. Pile the meringue on the dishes and return to the oven for about 10 minutes, or until brown and crisp. Garnish with a few raspberries or blackberries and a sprinkling of sugar. Serve slightly warm from the oven or at room temperature, and offer a dessert brandy for special occasions. *Dydd Santes Dwynwen Dda*—Happy Saint Dwynwen's Day! Serves 2 to 4.

Dwynwen's Monmouth Pudding and Raisin Stepony Wine

English Lemmone Syllabub (Custard)

ENGLISH RECIPE, CA. SIXTEENTH CENTURY

Syllabub custards have been popular since Tudor times. Although some might think of this tasty custard as purely Victorian in origin, it was also enjoyed in pre-colonial times. Inexpensive and easy to prepare, simple families would have enjoyed this on their holidays. Try this recipe with strong coffee or a snifter of brandy for an elegant example of our rich past.

Classic Lemmone Syllabub

Ingredients
2 cups whole goat or cow's milk
3/4 cup caster sugar, divided
1 tablespoon flour
4 eggs yolks
dash of ground cloves
1 teaspoon salt
⅓ cup sweet white wine
½ cup dark brandy
1 pint heavy cream
1 teaspoon vanilla extract
½ cup lemon zest

In a double boiler, bring the milk to a gentle boil. Mix half of the sugar with the flour and stir in the milk, then reduce heat to low and cook for 10 to 15 minutes, stirring constantly. Beat the egg yolks to a cream, adding the remaining sugar and the salt and clove powder, and continue to mix. Add the mixture to the hot milk and cook another 5 minutes, stirring. Remove from the heat and fold in the vanilla extract.

When the custard is slightly cool, pour into parfait glasses, fancy tumblers, or deep wine glasses to half full. Let it thicken in the refrigerator, then pour a thin layer of brandy on top of the custard, and return it to the refrigerator. In a separate bowl, whip the heavy cream with a whisk until thick and add the vanilla. Put a dollop of cream to each tumbler. Stir once and add the grated lemon peel. Serves 2 to 4.

Fruit Confit (Candied Fruit)
French/English recipe, ca. sixteenth century

Candied fruits and vegetables had adorned festive tables since medieval times. Offer these delectable treats with a fine dessert and tea or as an after-dinner nibble with a spiced Hippocras or Yuletide Wassail.

Candied Fruit and Raspberry Shrub

Ingredients
2 pounds assorted dried fruit (strawberries, apricots, cherries, figs, peaches, and/or pears)
2 oranges, whole or just the peels, sliced thin
2 lemons, whole or just the peels, sliced thin
1 stalk ginger, peeled and diced small
1½ cups water (depending on amount of fruit)
1 cup brown sugar
1 cup honey
1 tablespoon ground nutmeg
1 cup castor sugar or powdered sugar

Place the washed, pitted fruit and ginger in a crockpot with enough water to cover the fruit twice. Cover and cook on the lowest setting for 5 to 8 hours. Remove and let drain on a wire rack, then gently poke holes in each piece of fruit with a needle. In a deep pan, bring the water to a gentle boil. Add the brown sugar and honey and stir over medium-low heat until it becomes a thick syrup.

Add the fruit to the syrup, making sure each piece is thoroughly coated and translucent. Place each piece of fruit about 2 inches apart on wax paper until the sugar syrup hardens slightly.

In a clean jar, combine the nutmeg and castor sugar or powered sugar. Spoon the fruit into the jar, close the lid, and shake well. Put the powdered fruit in a large cookie tin filled with an inch or two of the powdered sugar spice. To serve, line a platter with paper doilies or powdered sugar and arrange the candied fruit on top. Garnish with edible flowers and dust with nutmeg or cinnamon. Serves 6 to 12.

Chapter 8. Herb, Root, and Spice
ZESTY TASTES TOO PIQUANT TO RESIST

"And all that's nice"—Andrew Marvell (1621-1678)

The spice box: spice rub, powder fine, powder douce, powder fort, bouqet garni, fines herbes

o historically authentic meal would be complete without the proper supply of spices and dried herbs. What follows is a sampling of the Paganus folks' most popular herbs and spices. Most of these recipes date back to at least the Dark Ages. They are intended to be used sparingly.

Spice Box
FRENCH/ENGLISH RECIPE, CA. FOURTEENTH CENTURY

The spice box was usually a copper, silver, or wooded box the size of a deck of playing cards. There would be several to a table and they would be filled for each meal. Use these sweet and spicy powders to enhance otherwise boring meals, or add to meat fillings for sausages and pies. This particular recipe is designed as a dry rub on roasts, fish, and vegetables, so you may use liberally. If you like, fry the spices in butter until it begins to smoke. When the butter has evaporated and the spices darken, let cool to a crust, and then grind again with a mortar and pestle.

Ingredients
½ cup ground sea salt
½ cup dried plain bread crumbs
1½ tablespoon raw or natural sugar
1 tablespoon ground cloves
1 tablespoon ground black pepper
1 tablespoon ground multi-colored pepper
1 tablespoon ground ginger
½ tablespoon ground mace
½ tablespoon ground cinnamon
½ tablespoon ground cardamom

Place all the ingredients in a large bowl and grind them to a fine powder. Place the spice mixture in a covered container, such as a wooded box or ceramic jar. When ready to serve at your meal, you may use these containers or place in bowls with small spoons. You may also offer this spice in small pinch bowls set at each place setting.

Spice Rub
SCOTTISH RECIPE, CA. FOURTEENTH CENTURY

This recipe uses the same ingredients as the basic spice box recipe, but calls for a strong, dark vinegar, cooking time, and fermentation time to create an authentic wet rub. Use this spice rub for basting wild duck and Cornish hens or for roasting capons and other game meats.

Ingredients
½ cup ground sea salt
1 tablespoon ground cloves
1 tablespoon ground black pepper
1 tablespoon ground multi-colored pepper
1 tablespoon ground ginger
½ tablespoon ground mace

½ tablespoon ground cinnamon
½ tablespoon ground cardamom
½ cup dried plain bread crumbs
4 cups red wine vinegar
1½ tablespoon raw or natural sugar

Combine the salt, spices, bread crumbs, vinegar, and sugar in a large saucepan and simmer on low heat for 15 to 20 minutes. Let cool, then pour the unstrained liquid into empty wine bottles. Cork and place in the refrigerator for a week or so before use. This will bring out the natural flavors. When ready to use, shake the bottle vigorously and pour liberally over meats and vegetables while cooking. If roasting large game birds, continue to saturate with the spice rub while cooking.

Powder Fine
FRENCH/ENGLISH RECIPES, CA. FOURTEENTH CENTURY

This recipe can be found in one form or another in ancient cookbooks dating to the fourteenth century. During the crusades, mixed spices like powder fine, powder douce, and powder fort were commonly used throughout Europe to give meats and fish a unique flavor. Offer these delightful spices in individual pinch bowls or spice boxes with small spoons. You may wish to arrange a sample of these spices on a platter along with your feast for show and added flavor.

Ingredients
3 tablespoons ground ginger
2 to 4 tablespoons ground cinnamon
1 tablespoon ground cloves
1 tablespoon grains of paradise

Combine the spices and grind them with a mortar and pestle to create a fine dust. Sprinkle over meats and fish, and use in sausage. Keep in an airtight container when not in use.

Powder Douce
FRENCH/ENGLISH RECIPE, CA. FOURTEENTH CENTURY

Though originally used for meats and fish, this spice mixture works exceedingly well as a topping for desserts and pastries, or in butter spreads. Add sugar to make a wonderful sprinkle for hot, buttered toast.

Ingredients
4 tablespoons light brown sugar
1 to 2 tablespoons ground coriander
2 tablespoons ground cinnamon

Combine the spices and grind them with a mortar and pestle to create a fine dust. Sprinkle over ground meats and vegetables. Keep in an airtight container when not in use.

Powder Fort

FRENCH/ENGLISH RECIPE, CA. FIFTEENTH CENTURY

This spiced powder is perfect for fish dishes and most seafood. It also goes well on hot buttered biskets and scrambled eggs.

Ingredients
1 tablespoon ground cumin
5 to 6 tablespoons ground black pepper
2 tablespoons ground ginger

Combine the sugar and spices and grind them with a mortar and pestle to create a fine dust. Keep in an airtight container when not in use.

Bouquet Garni

FRENCH RECIPE, CA. SIXTEENTH CENTURY

Bouquet garni, or "garnished bouquet," is a collection of fresh or dried herbs for cooking. Many chefs, myself included, prefer fresh herbs, as they release natural juices to the recipe. Basically, tie the herbs in a bunch like a bouquet of flowers and let them drift in a pot of soup, stew, or broth, or add to roasted or broiled pungent meats like mutton or lamb shank. They are tied together so they can be removed easily at the end of the cooking process. Many cooks will also add basil, burnet, chervil, rosemary, and tarragon, as well as vegetables such as carrots, celery, celeriac, leeks, and green onions. Bouquet garni can be purchased online or in fine restaurant-grocers across the globe, though it's just as easy to prepare at home.

Ingredients
3 sprigs fresh thyme
3 sprigs fresh savory
2 large fresh or dried bay leaves
5 sprigs fresh parsley

Tie the fresh herbs together with cooking string or household all-natural fiber string, and freeze for up to a month, or use fresh for best results. Discard after using.

Fines Herbes

According to Julia Child in *Mastering the Art of French Cooking,* fines herbes is the culinary mainstay in French cuisine and is practically as old as the French culture. The ingredients are a combination of fresh herbs, such as parsley, chives, tarragon, and chervil. Less pungent than those found in the bouquet garni, fines herbes are designed to release their unique flavors during the long cooking process of stews, soups, and sauces. This recipe calls for fresh herbs, though dried works well, too.

Ingredients
5 sprigs fresh parsley
4 sprigs fresh chervil
4 sprigs fresh sweet cicely
4 sprigs fresh marjoram
4 sprigs fresh tarragon
4 sprigs fresh watercress
4 sprigs fresh lemon balm

Finely chop the fresh herbs. If you use a food processor, avoid mashing the herbs. Fines herbes are meant to be almost invisible to best blend with the foods. I make only enough for each recipe, because the stored mixture loses the distinctive flavors. Add the fines herbes to soups, sauces, and stuffing served with seafood, lamb, and veal.

Chapter 9. Sauces and Vinegars
RICH OR LIGHT, THICK OR THIN,
CONDIMENTS SERVED TO FRIENDS AND KIN

"Mild or bold, fit for young and old."
—Song of Solomon 4:16, KJV 1611

Sixteenth-century image from the 1526 book, *The Grete Herball. Courtesy of Society for Creative Anachronism, Arts and Sciences of the Middle Ages and Renaissance*

Although many of the ancient recipes in this book are already spicy and rich, sauces and compotes were customary. The following recipes were popular during the fifth through the sixteenth centuries, and I have included a small selection of traditional recipes used by Paganus peoples since ancient times. They are well-suited to meats, fowl, and fish, and can be used interchangeably or served condiment-style in small bowls.

Verjuice (Green Juice)
FRENCH/ENGLISH RECIPE, CA. THIRTEENTH CENTURY

Known as vertjus and Pinot Noir verjus to the French, this semi-bitter vinegar is used primarily for roasting, scalding, and baking, but also for sauces, vinaigrettes, and compotes. Verjuice is essentially the pressings of unripe grapes and green crabapples known as agraz. Verjuice is available at specialty grocers, but you can make your own with relative ease.

Ingredients
1 pound unripe grapes, gooseberries, or green apples
1 crabapple, or 5 tablespoons of bottled juice
10 to 15 sorrel leaves
2 cups white vinegar
½ cup dry white wine

Combine the fruit and sorrel leaves in a food processor. Grind to a pulp, spread the mixture on a cheesecloth, and strain into a large jar, discarding the pulp. Add the wine and vinegar and shake. Cap the bottle and place in a cool, dark place for 2 or 3 weeks. Strain through another piece of cheesecloth into a tall, empty wine bottle and refrigerate for future use. Use liberally for basting game birds and game meats like deer, boar, and bear, and for sauces to add a little bite. For an exotic flavor, add a few tablespoons of verjuice to fruit salads and fresh fruit dishes.

Leek Sauce
ENGLISH RECIPE, CA. FIFTEENTH CENTURY

This simple yet hearty sauce is best served over heavy or pungent game meats such as wild boar and venison. It also works with steamed vegetables, like green beans, wild peas, carrots, and field greens.

Ingredients
4 large leeks
4 cups beef or vegetable broth
2 strips bacon (optional)
½ cup ground almonds
½ teaspoon pepper, coarsely ground

Wash the leeks well, cut off and discard the green husk, and chop the white part into thin slivers. In a saucepan, place the leeks in the broth along with a few slices of bacon, and bring to a rolling boil. After a few minutes, reduce heat to low and simmer for 20 minutes, until all is tender. Strain the liquid into a bowl and remove the leeks and bacon, placing them aside. Add the ground almonds to the broth and return it to a simmer until the broth is thick. In a food processor, grind the leeks and the bacon to a semi-fine paste. Scoop this into the broth, cover, and continue simmering for another 20 to 30 minutes. Serve hot in a side dish or gravy boat.

Garlic Sauce
English recipe, ca. sixteenth century

The use of garlic in food preparation dates back before biblical times and has never fallen out of grace. During America's colonial period, garlic was used to flavor roasts, baked foods, stews, and of course sauces. This ancient recipe works best on pungent meats, but also nicely tops chicken, beef, and fish dishes.

Ingredients
5 tablespoons butter
10 to 15 garlic cloves, pureed
3 tablespoons white flour
1 cup whole milk
½ tablespoon sea salt
½ tablespoon pepper
¼ teaspoon ground saffron or paprika

In a medium-sized saucepan, melt the butter slowly, add the pureed garlic, and whisk in the flour until creamy. Add the milk and continue to whisk. As the sauce begins to bubble a bit, add the salt, pepper, and saffron, reduce the heat to low, and simmer for 15 to 25 minutes, stirring. If you wish, add more flour to make it thicker. Serves 4 to 8.

Composta (Sweet Vinaigrette)
Spanish/French recipe, ca. sixteenth century

This simple recipe of cooked vegetables and roots can be added to any sweet vinaigrette. Add this lively sauce to stews, soups, over meats, and on salads. Composta also goes well as a dipping sauce for breads when mixed with olive oil.

Ingredients
6 parsley roots
3 parsnips
3 carrots
10 radishes
3 turnips
1 head cabbage
5 tablespoons olive oil
3 cups water
1 large pear, sliced
1 red apple, sliced
½ tablespoon sea salt

1 tablespoon pepper
1 cup red wine vinegar
1 tablespoon ground mustard
1 tablespoon ground paprika
1 tablespoon ground cinnamon
1 tablespoon whole anise seed
1 tablespoon whole fennel seed
1 cup sweet red wine
½ cup clover honey
1½ cups red currants or raisins

Wash, peel, and dice the vegetables into small chunks. Using a large, deep pan or fryer, add the olive oil and water and boil for 10 minutes until the vegetables are tender. Add the sliced pear and apple, cover, and simmer for 25 minutes. Drain the water and set aside. Put the cooked vegetables in a large bowl. Add the salt, pepper, vinegar, and spices and mix well. Cover and refrigerate overnight. Bring the mixture to room temperature. In a saucepan, bring the wine and honey to a light boil, then cover and simmer for 10 minutes. Turn off the heat and remove any froth from the surface. When cool, add the red currants or raisins and stir well. Pour over the cold vegetables. Serve 12 to 20.

Mahonesa (Mediterranean-style Salad Dressing)
MINORCAN RECIPE, CA. SEVENTEENTH AND EIGHTEENTH CENTURIES

Originally from the Balearic Islands in the Mediterranean, Mahonesa salad dressing is basically simple mayonnaise. It is best used over folk herb salats, heart-of-palm salads, or over greens. Add fresh dill if you wish.

  1 cup light olive oil
  1 egg yolk
  juice of 1 lemon
  2 tablespoon white vinegar
  salt and pepper, to taste 2 sprigs fresh basil leaves

In a bowl, combine the olive oil, egg yolk, lemon juice, and vinegar, and whip with a whisk or hand blender until thick. Fold in the salt and pepper. Pour over the salad or serve the dressing in a separate bowl, along with minced basil leaves. Serves 3 to 6.

Herbal Butter Sauce
FRENCH RECIPE, CA. FIFTEENTH CENTURY

The Huguenots were making this time-honored culinary delight long before they landed on the shores of the new world. This easy butter sauce is perfect for warm breads and potato and pasta dishes, and for adding richness to bland meat dishes. When presenting a feast of many dishes, off it in a separate dish or LaRochere glassware as a sign of your culinary knowledge.

1 cup butter
½ cup heavy whipping cream
1 teaspoon sea salt
4 tablespoons dried dill
2 tablespoons ground pepper

Let the butter soften naturally, and then stir in the heavy cream until well-mixed. Add the sea salt, dill, and pepper, and transfer to a serving dish. Refrigerate until ready to use. If using as a sauce for meats, gently simmer in a saucepan until ready to pour. Add a variety of seasonal herbs to make a delightful and tasty addition to any meal. Serves 8 to 12.

Honey and Spice Butter
ENGLISH RECIPE, CA. SIXTEENTH CENTURY

Here is yet another spice popular during the Elizabethan age, when sweet cakes and heavy creams graced the tables of most homesteads, and where no morsel was left barren of a sauce, cheese, or compote of some sort. Sweet butters and sauces like this one would have been used for spreads on biscuits and breads, but also for meats like chicken and fish, so feel free to add it to almost any meal, as our ancestors once did to brighten their days.

1 cup whole butter
½ cup flower honey
½ cup sour cream
4 tablespoons ground cinnamon
2 teaspoons ground nutmeg
1 teaspoon ground white pepper

Use fresh honey and the freshest-churned butter you can find, such as a pure salted or unsalted Irish butter made from the milk of grass fed cows. If you can't make your own, Kerrygold is a high-quality brand of butter and cheese. Mix the softened butter with the honey, sour cream, and the spices until uniform in color. Store in the refrigerator until ready to use. You will never look at ordinary butter the same way.

Making Cheese, woodcut by Schweizer Chronik, by J. Stumpf, 1548. *Courtesy of Society for Creative Anachronism*

Conclusion

And so completes our brief look into the world of ancient cooking techniques, Paganus celebrations and festivities, and the foods and libations these unique peoples consumed. Our ancient ancestors honored their gods and goddesses with as much color and joy as any faith congregation today, if not more.

Ancient Paganus peoples often poured honey and fresh milk into the just-tilled ground to show gratitude and gain favor for the crop to come. When that crop arrived, if it fell on a feast day or when a solstice celebration was being prepared, great bales of wheat and barley, oats, and flowers were offered as a sacrifice, as was milk and fruit. When the time came to offer their joyous odes, they sang and danced and carried on in the most excitable manner imaginable. The goal was to give thanks for life-sustaining food, but also to give praise to their fellow women and men for helping the community thrive. This practice is part of the culinary history of every nation on earth.

It might amaze us that the ancient Egyptians were among the first to make beer as a result of their experimentation with hops and grains. The ancient Vikings, Celts, and Germanic peoples discovered just how delicious fermented honey could be, creating outstanding meads and Chouchen wines. The Celts figured out how to make apple and pear ciders that kept them warm during the winter months, beginning a tradition that continues to this day. Such recipes mark an ingenuity that has traveled through time and a tenacious determination to remember the past. This is the very foundation of the human condition, for which we should all be proud.

In the tradition of making gods and goddesses into edible effigies as a sign of respect, we can see similarities between the old religion and modern faiths such as Christianity, Judaism, and Islam. While each has their dogmas and mannerisms, they are more related than we often perceive. For example, our ancestors celebrated Lammas, which means *hlaf-maesse*, or loaf-mass, a ritual of gratitude for grains and the harvest. This is similar to the Holy Communion that many modern faiths observe. While the bread-like wafer represents Christ's flesh for modern Christians, ancient Paganus folk consumed bread with an effigy of a man, or god, baked on the top in the hope of a good harvest in the year ahead. We are all connected to the same tether, whether we like it or not.

It's true that the idea of eating some of the things our ancestors relished, such as sauced hedgehog and blackbird pie, would make us feel sick today. Yet so many of their recipes are quite at home on a modern menu. In the realm of folklore this is simply known as oral tradition passed down from family to family or community to community. As our medieval ancestors honored gods from the Greek, Roman, Celtic, and polytheistic traditions, so too modern peoples value their ancestors' most honorable traditions. I invite you to use these recipes to honor the seasons, your friends and family, and most of all, yourself, with the joy of knowing that all you do reflects the humble beginnings of our ancient families.

May blessing find you and keep you all the year long!

Appendices

Appendix A. Register of Herbs and Spices

This listing of herbs, spices, and edible flowers represents some of the most common varieties used in ancient cooking. As you explore cooking methods for creating your feast, consider the flavors of the meats, fish, vegetables, and fruits you plan on using. For instance, sweet and spicy fish and fowl dishes work well served on a bed of slightly bitter flower petals and herbs such as calendula or lovage, as they balance the flavors. Colorful herbs like dill and borage will bring flair to otherwise bland foods and sauces. Use the herbs and spices with the recipes in this book.

Herbs, Plants, and Seeds

Angelica (*Angelica* sp.)
Although used as a medicinal, this herb is excellent for stews and soups. Try sprinkling a handful in a cabbage soup or use it as a bed for roast game bird.

Anise (*Pimpinella*)
The sweet taste of anise has flavored cookies and cakes for centuries, and is an excellent oil or powder for spicy recipes, too. Add a drop or two to meat stews and roasts for a uniquely English taste, or add to base liquors for a Spanish drink.

Lemon balm (*Melissa officinalis*)
An excellent herb to add to soups and teas. Especially good for colds and flu, this herb is said to speed recovery.

Basic (*Ocimum*)
Genovese sweet, purple ruffle, licorice, lemon, and the many other varieties of this delightfully potent herb will enhance any bland meal. Add the fresh herb to salads and salsas for an extra zing, or the dried herb to sauces and roasting meats.

Bergamot (*Monarda didyma*)
An excellent herb for stews, meat pies, and casseroles. The leaves' slightly pungent flavor complements sweet side dishes.

Borage (*Borago officinalis*)
Use fresh borage leaves for sweet meat dishes, such as chicken and fish, and in salads and sandwiches. Try this in dark teas for an authentic eighteenth-century beverage.

Calendula (*Calendula officinalis*)
Excellent for teas and soups, this herb adds an earthy flavor without being too pungent.

Caraway (*Carum carvi*)
Use the seed for breads and meat pies, but use sparely, as it can overtake other flavors.

Chamomile (*Matricaria recutita*)
Of the many classifications, this flowery herb, whether German or Roman variety, has been used as an important medicinal for centuries. Use as a tea or in a hot bath when sick. Add to roast meats such as beef, boar or bear to absorb gamy oils.

Chervil (*Anthriscus cerefolium*)
A mainstay herb in French cooking, chervil is excellent in stews and as a primary herb in vinegars and compotes. Works will with dill for fish dishes.

Chives (*Allium schoenoprasum*)
Use mild chives for pasta, potato and other starchy dishes. The gentle green earth flavor will invigorate bland dishes, as well as add color.

Coriander (*Coriandrum sativum*)
Much like cilantro, use this herb in similar methods. Try this herb with the garlic sauce recipe for color and texture.

Cumin (*Cuminum cyminum*)
Much like the anise seed, cumin adds the exotic flavor of ancient Egypt when applied to meat dishes. Add this seed in meat pies and sausages for a spicy flavor cherished by the English for centuries.

Dill (*Anethum graveolens*)
Excellent for any fish dish, try this herb with seafood casseroles, clam bakes or any fish chowders. Use the yellow flowers of the dill weed as an herb to season soups and dips and the seeds for pickling and baking.

Fennel (*Foeniculum vulgare*)
The sweet fennel seed, when crushed, is an excellent anti-fungal and makes for a delightful toothpaste. When added to foods such as bread and cookies, or fish dishes, you'll get an exotic and airy flavor.

Fenugreek (*Trigonella foenumgraeum*)
Great in fresh salads and chutneys, also add this to meats if boiling. This will give a gentle earthy flavor to many meat and fish dishes.

Horehound, white (*Marrubium vulgare*)
A remedy for sore throats and hoarseness, horehound also makes a delightful tea with after-dinner sweets.

Hyssop, blue (*Hyssopus officinalis*)
Considered a holy herb and used by early people for cleansing and bathing, hyssop also makes an excellent tea when sick or feeling under the weather. Try using the fresh or dried herb in chicken soups to add flavor and purify the system.

Lavender, (*Lavandula vera*)
A mainstay of everything French, lavender petals are used in everything from light broths to cordials to cosmetics and candies. Lavender truly is a wonder herb that will always add to the dinner table.

Lemongrass (*Cymbopogon*)
Use lemongrass in teas and light broths for a unique citrus flavor that will add to most wild game dishes.

Lemon verbena (*Aloysia triphylla*)
Try verbena extract or essence in baked goods such as breads and cookies for a light, unique citrus flavor.

Licorice (*Glycyrrhiza glabra*)
True licorice has a flavor similar to anise seed but is slightly more bitter. Use this as an extract for mixed drinks.

Lovage (*Levisticum officinale*)
This perennial herb imparts a celery-type flavor to beef stews and soups. Try lightly frying this herb with watercress and parsley, and then spreading it on baked game birds for a hearty flavor.

Marjoram, sweet (*Origanum majorana)*
Use the freshly chopped herb in salads for a little sweetness and on fried fish with dill for color and taste.

Mint (*Mentha*)
Whether peppermint, bergamot mint, pennyroyal, spearmint, apple or pineapple mint varieties, these delightfully potent herbs will brighten up beverages such as teas and alcohol drinks, but also add flavor to meat and fish dishes. Add this herb to summer salads and grind into salsas.

Mustard (*Brassica*)
Black, brown, white and yellow mustards have specific uses: for fresh green salads and stews or dried and powdered and added to sauces. Fresh mustard greens also make a nice bedding on platters.

Oregano, European (*Origanum vulgare*)
Use freshly chopped oregano for salads and platter bedding, or the dried herb for sauces and stews. Oregano imparts a slightly bitter, but soft, earthy taste to pesto sauces and compotes.

Parsley (*Petroselinum hortense*)
Enjoyed for centuries, use fresh parsley as a topping for sauces, and dried for pastas and other starches, and for fried seafood.

Rosemary (*Rosmarinus officinalis*)
Use this delightfully pungent herb for broiled lamb dishes and other game animals. When added with dark or stone-ground mustard, rosemary creates a unique taste for baked or broiled meats.

Saffron (*Crocus sativus*)
The pollen strands of the crocus flower, saffron is costly to cultivate and buy. Honored since ancient times, saffron was considered gold to cooks and an object of status for kings and queens around the world. Use saffron sparely on the delicate foods and drinks. If used only for coloring, substitute paprika.

Sage (*Salvia officinales*)
Considered the herb of the wise, pungent sage offers a heavy flavor for meats and stews, and is oddly light in fresh salads. Try sage in meat pies made with lamb, kidney, or beef.

Savory (*Calamintha*)
Use savory for stews, salads, and seafood dishes.

Tarragon (*Artemisia dracunculus sativa*)
Another well-respected French herb, its potent flavor is best used in bland chicken and egg dishes. Use dried tarragon in salads or as a topping for pasta dishes.

Thyme (*Thymus vulgaris*)
Both English and French varieties have many noble purposes. It may be used as a tea for indigestion and sore throat, as a dried sprinkle for eggs and cream sauces, and for roast meats and fish dishes. You may also use the fresh herb in salads and compotes.

Valerian (*Valeriana officinalis*)
When used as a tea, the earthy valerian root has a stringent effect on the skin and lulls one to sleep when mixed with chamomile and skullcap. For culinary use, add a little of the leaf to meat pies to work in consort with sweet ingredients, such as nutmeg and cinnamon.

Wintergreen (*Gaultheria procumbens*)
Use the wintergreen leaves in lamb stews and meat pies containing lamb. Add a little of the fresh herb to cocktails and sangria for an extra zing.

Edible Flowers

Edible flowers would have been used in only the most festive occasions, such as wedding banquets, coronation feasts, and for visiting dignitaries. Paganus peoples depended on many varieties of flowers for food itself. Try a bouquet of sugar-dusted violets with a spicy wine, or pine nut and dandelion basil pesto for a zesty chicken dish. Use only the freshest flowers, and only those that have not been sprayed with insecticides.

Arugula, also called rocket, is an Italian green used in salads and sandwiches. The small flowers are white with dark centers and are excellent in salads. The leaves range in color from white to yellow with dark purple and resemble radish leaves. The natural spicy flavor is best accented with a light vinaigrette and ground black pepper.

Burnet leaf tastes like cucumber and works well with borage and spinach.

Calendula, or marigolds, are one of the tastiest flowers available. Ranging from spicy to bitter or peppery, and slightly resembling saffron, they can be used as a substitute for certain spices. Sprinkle the fresh or dried flower on soups, pastas, and rice dishes and add the whole flowers as garnishes. You may even use the flowers in herbal butters for flavor and color, and in egg dishes and in salads for a rich, exotic taste.

Carnations are one of the most common edible flowers. Candied and used as decorations on cakes and pies, or as a candy, the carnation has an exotic taste yet is not overpowering. Steep the fresh, washed flower in a choice wine for several weeks, strain, and serve as an exotic garden nectar. For dessert, simply cut off the stems and white base, wash, and dust in a triple powder and spice such as nutmeg; let dry and serve as is. Try serving a carnation salad with a glass of the French liqueur Chartreuse, a wonderful drink made of the delicate carnation. This flower has served royalty and commoners since the early seventeenth century.

Chicory adds a pleasant, mildly bitter taste to a salad of arugula and watercress. Dress with a light vinaigrette and lemon.

Chrysanthemums offer a tangy, yet slightly bitter flavor, and are best used in green leafy salads or with a roast of game bird. Blanch the flowers first, discarding the stems and base caps. Scatter the petals over the salad or roast, and serve.

Clover offers a slightly sweet flavor close to licorice, with just a hint of bitterness. Use clover sparingly on fish dishes and salads.

Dandelions are likely the sweetest flowers available, especially when picked young. The honey flavor of the young flower makes a nice addition to dessert dishes like cakes and tarts, as well as to wines. Sprinkle the fresh flowers over steamed rice for a festive and colorful dish.

Daylilies, a unique variety of the lily flower, serve several purposes. Their slightly sweet, vegetable-like flavor adds a hint of fresh melon to lettuce salads. Use the sweet petals in desserts for color and texture, and the flowers on salad platters for a delightful crowning effect. (Daylilies have a laxative effect, so use sparingly.)

English daisies are mildly bitter flowers that taste of kosher pickles and go delightfully well with salads. Use only the petal in salad combinations or sprinkle over rice and soups.

Fuchsia flowers have little taste but make an excellent garnish for large platters. Decorate a roast chicken or turkey or float on top of large bowls of soup for a royal look.

Gardenia, a highly scented flower known for jazzing up jasmine teas in the Far East, also offers an excellent garnish for pungent dishes such as fish. They also make wonderful floaters on large bowls of soups and bisques.

Garden sorrel offers a light, tangy taste that accompanies spicy foods nicely. Use the petals in tomato sauces and in watercress and cucumber salads for a little zing.

Geranium offers a slightly bitter taste that's great for balancing sweeter salads and hot teas. Try adding geranium and rose petals to sweet batter to make tasty muffins fit for a king or queen.

Gladiola flowers have a dull flavor almost like lettuce, yet they're good in savory butter and cream cheese spreads and for topping rich mousses. Use the petals in tomato and cucumber salads.

Hibiscus flowers, with a slight acidic, tangy flavor resembling oranges and cranberries, are an excellent addition for most salads. Sprinkle over fish and fowl dishes for something different.

Jasmine flowers are rich in color and fragrance and work well for scenting teas and soups and adding color to exotic stews and fish dishes.

Lilac flowers have a slightly bitter flavor that nicely complements many dishes. Its lemon flavor, with just a hint of floral, works especially well in salads and fish dishes.

Linden flowers have small, yellowish petals that are delightfully fragrant and sweet. The honey-like flavor contributes to sauces, butter and cheese spreads, and pungent dishes. Sprinkle over fruit platters to add elegance for parties and other royal engagements.

Marjoram flowers are mild and largely tasteless, but their rich color makes a memorable presentation as garnishes on hot and cold soups and game roasts.

Pansies offer a sweet, grassy flavor with just the hint of wintergreen. Add the petals to soups, fruit salads, and desserts for color and taste.

Queen Anne's Lace has a carrot-like flavor that works well in salads and vegetable soups.

Radish flowers, much like the radish itself, have a pungent, spicy flavor. The flowers are white, pink, or yellowish, and work well in green, leafy salads and hearty stews.

Rose petals, depicting love, honor, and royalty, have a vibrant flavor similar to sour apples and strawberries, with mint undertones. All roses are edible, so use any variety to flavor your food. Use the miniature varieties to garnish cream desserts and parfaits. Sprinkle the petals over salads and soups, and freeze them in ice cubes to float on festive sangrias and punches. You may even use the petals in jellies, syrups, butters, and breads. Garnish sorbets and Italian ices, or sugar-crystallize the petals for delightful candies.

Safflower hearts, also referred to as Spanish saffron, is used primarily to color foods, but also serve as a splendid aromatic for spicy and bitter dishes. Use this flower and its rhizomes for lighting up large platters of roast meats, sausages, and fish.

Tulip petals, with a flavor of sweet lettuce or cucumber, make a wonderful accompaniment to fish dishes and steamed asparagus. Sprinkle over green leafy salads and hot soups for a pleasant lift.

Violets are sweet and aromatic, and their tender leaves and flowers are an attractive addition to a salad. Use any variety to embellish desserts, hot teas, and cold drinks. Freeze the petals in ice cubes to liven up punch and adorn cakes, iced creams, and sorbets.

Appendix B. International Cheese Sellers

These reliable cheese companies offer some of the best and most authentic cheeses on the market today, whether you're looking for Caerffili, Cenarth brie, Perl Las, or oak-smoked garlic and herb cheeses. If in doubt, you can email these cheese sellers for information and advice, as they are the experts on all things cheese. Of course, you can always visit your neighborhood gourmet grocer or world market for a good selection of cheeses from around the world.

United Kingdom

Bermic Cheese Specialists—Maidenhead
Tel.: 01628 829911

Briddlesford Lodge—Wooton
Tel.: 01983 884650
www.briddlesfordlodgefarm.co.uk

Caracoli—Alresford
Tel.: 01962 738730
www.caracoli.co.uk

Caws Cenarth Cheese
Glyneithinog Farm, Pontseli, Boncath,
Dyfed, SA37 0LH
Wales, United Kingdom
Tel.: +44(0)1239 710432
email: cenarth.cheese@virgin.net

Chale Green Stores—Chale Green
Tel.: 01983 551201
www.chalegreenstores.co.uk

Cheese at Leadenhall—EC3
Tel.: 0207 9291697
www.cheeseatleadenhall.co.uk

Crumbs of Sussex
Tel.: 01903 891603
www.crumbsofsussex.co.uk

Farmer Jack's—Arreton Barns
Tel.: 01983 527530
www.farmerjacks.co.uk

Longman's Cheese Sales Ltd.—Yeovil
Tel.: 01963 441146
www.longman-cheese-sales.co.uk

Love Local—Botley
Tel.: 01489 783614
www.love-local.co.uk

Old Farmhouse Bakery
Tel.: 01235 831230
www.theoldfarmhousebakery.co.uk

Pembrokeshire Cheese Company
Pembroke Road, Merlins Bridge,
Haverfordwest, Pembrokeshire SA61 1JN
Tel.: 01978 782 365

Priory Farmshop—South Nutfield
Tel.: 01737 822603
www.prioryfarm.co.uk

Queen Bower Caravan Park Dairy
Alverstone Road, Sandown
Isle of Wight, PO36 0NZ
Tel.: 01983 403840
Fax: 01983 409671
www.queenbowerdairy.co.uk
email: queenbowerdairy@btconnect.com

Rippon Cheeses—SW1
Tel.: 0207 9310628
www.ripponcheese.com (Berkshire)

Rowan's Delicatessen—Petersfield
Tel.: 01730 262600
www.rowansdeli.co.uk

Snowdonia Cheese Company
Unit B6, Trem y Dyffryn, Colomendy
Industrial Estate
Denbigh, LL16 5TX, UK

Tel.: 00 44 (0)1745 813388
Fax: 00 44 (0)1745 813550
email: sales@snowdonia-cheese.co.uk

The Isle of Wight Cheese Company Ltd
Alverstone Road, Sandown
Isle of Wight PO36 0NZ, United Kingdom
Tel.: 01983 402736
email: rich@isleofwightcheese.co.uk

The Garlic Farm—Newchurch
Tel.: 01983 865378
www.thegarlicfarm.co.uk

Three Gates Farm Shop—Shalfleet
Tel.: 01983 531204
www.capoundourneclassics.co.uk

Warborne Farmshop—Boldre, Lymington
Tel.: 01590 688488
www.warbornefarm.co.uk

Spain

Here's a selection of authentic cheeses that use goat, cow, sheep, and mixed milks in their cheeses. Some types were used in recipes that may well have been served to El Cid himself. These companies have English-language websites. Though many of these cheeses are very rich and will work perfectly with the Spanish dishes in this book, they are also delicious alone or with fruits, traditional sangrias, and wines.

Among some of the most popular and historically accurate cheeses are tetilla and San Simon, lighter cheeses from the Galicia region. Arzua-ulloa, also from Galicia, is a medium-sharp cheese. Mahon, from the Balearic Islands, and Izbores goat's milk cheese from Extremadura, are also good examples of medium-flavored Spanish cheeses. Among the more pungent and stronger cheeses are Manchego, a sheep's milk cheese from Castilla-La Mancha, Roncal from Navarra, Zamorano from Castilla-Leon, and Idiazabal, from the Basque Country regions. All are excellent examples of stronger cheeses that will consort well with most of the Spanish dishes in this book. Many of these cheeses can also be found in fine grocers.

Avda. Levante
53-Enlo. 9 "Edif. Geminis" 30520 Jumilla, Murcia
Tel.:34 968 783 804
Fax: 34 968 783 796

Cabrales
33555-Carreña de Cabrales, Principado de Asturias
Tel.: 34 985 845 335
Fax: 34 985 845 130
Email: fundacion@quesocabrales.org
Web: http://www.quesocabrales.org/

Gamonedo
Consejería de Medio Rural y Pesca del Principado de Asturias
(Asturias Council for Fishing and Rural Land)
C/ Coronel Aranda, s/n 33005 - Oviedo, Asturias.

Tel.: 34 985 105 637
Fax: 34 985 105 517

Ibores
Mercado Regional de GanadoC/ Ctra. de Madrid, s/n 10200
Trujillo, Cáceres.
Tel. and fax: 34 927 323 0 76
Web: http://www.cabraibores.com

Idiazabal
Granja Modelo Arkaute, 01080 Vitoria-Gasteiz, Alava
Tel.: 34 945 289 971
Fax: 34 945 281422
Web: http://www.quesoidiazabal.com

L'Alturgell
C/ Sant Ermengol, 37, 25700 La Seu D'Urgell (Lleida)
Tel.: 34 973 350 266 - Fax: 34 973 352 705

Mahon
Ctra. D`es Grau Km. 0,5 07700 Mahón,
Baleares
Tel.: 34 971 362 295 Fax: 34 971 368 260
Email: quesomahon@infoTel.:ecom.es
Web: http://www.quesomahonmenorca.com

Majorero
Avda. Primero de May, 59, 35600 Puerto
del Rosario–
Fuerteventura, Las Palmas, Islas Canarias
Tel. and fax: 34 928 532 593

Nata de Cantabria
C/ Héroes 2 de Mayo, 27, 39600
Muriendas, Cantabria
Tel.: 34 942 269 855
Web: http://www.alimentosdecantabria.com

Roncal
Carretera del Sadar, s/n. Edif. El Sario,
31006 Pamplona, Navarra
Tel.: 34 948 238 512
Fax: 34 948 232 070
Email: iconsejo@nacersa.com
Web: http://www.denominacionesnavarra.
com/queso/portader.htm

Tetilla
Pazo de Quián–Sergude, 15881 Boqueixón,
La Coruña
Tel.: 34 981 511 751
Fax: 34 981 511 864
Email: quesotetilla@hotmail.com

Zamorano
C/ Cardenal Mella, 7, 49009 Zamora –
Spain. Tel.:. & Fax: 34 980 511 715
Email: denominacion@quesounceamorano.com

Palmero

C/ Europa, 3, 38710 - Beña Alta, La Palma
- (S.C.Tenerife)
Tel.: 34 922 417 060
Fax: 34 922 417 060
Web: http://www.quesopalmero.es
Email: quesopalmero@quesopalmero.es Picón

Cantabria, Picón y Quesucos de Liebana
C/ Héroes 2 de Mayo, 27, 39600
Muriendas, Cantabria
Tel.: 34 942 269 855
Web: http://www.alimentosdecantabria.com/

France

Throughout France, rounds of Vacherin appear only in winter, while buttons of chèvre, made with goat's cheese and coated in cumin, paprika, pepper, raisins, nuts, cinnamon, and caraway, are prepared year-round. There's always a raw milk camembert or heady brie or blue cheese available from these French suppliers and boutiques, which offer bulk products from small platters perfect for dinner parties to large trays for opulent banquets. Many of these shops also stock small selections of wines, jams, biscuits, and chutney.

The primary cheeses are: Petit Suisse, Brousse, Brie, Camembert, Chaource, and Reblochon Cheese, and hundreds more of every type and flavor. Remember, the French like their food, and as you would any fine painting or perfume from this land, expect to pay handsomely—it is usually well worth the investment.

Alain Boulay, Fromagerie Mouffetard
131, rue Mouffetard, 75005 Paris
Tel.: 01-47-07-18-15
Proprietor: Alain Boulay Censier-
Daubenton

Androuët
Address: 37, rue de Verneuil, 75007 Paris
Tel.: 01-42-61-97-55, 01-42-61-97-56

Androuët sur le Pouce (fromagerie/
restaurant)
134, rue Mouffetard, 75005 Paris
Tel.: 01-45-87-85-05

Censier-Daubenton
Ferme Sainte-Hyacinth, Fromagerie du
Panthéon
198, rue Saint-Jacques, 75005 Paris
Tel.: 01-43-54-68-32

Crémerie des Carmes
47 ter, boulevard St-Germain, 75005 Paris

Concorde
Fromagerie Corvetto
Address: 8, rue Corvetto, 75008 Paris
Tel.: 01-45-63-45-17, Villiers

Fromagerie Cler SARL
Address: 31, rue Cler, 75007 Paris
Tel.: 01-47-05-48-95

Fromagerie/Crémerie Quatrehomme
Address: 62, rue de Sèvres, 75007 Paris
Tel.: 01-47-34-33-45

Fromages et Détail (cheese shop chain, five
in Paris)
38, rue Cler, 75007 Paris
Tel.: 01-45-55-08-64, École Militaire, La
Tour-Maubourg

Fromage Rouge Fromagerie Saint-Do
83, rue Saint-Dominique, 75007 Paris
Tel.: 01-45-50-45-7
Email: fromagerouge@club-internet.fr

La Fermerie (épicerie, fromagerie, restaurant)
24, rue Surcouf, 75007 Paris
Tel.: 01-45-55-23-03
Email: contact@lafermerie.com
Web: http://www.lafermerie.com/en/
boutiques_cafe.html

La Fromagerie 31
64, rue de Seine, 75006 Paris
Tel.: 01-43-26-50-31

La Fromagerie de Grenelle, Chez Nathalie
Address: 204, rue de Grenelle, 75007 Paris
Tel.: 01-45-51-57-59,

La Tour Maubourg
Fromageries Bel
4, rue d'Anjou, 75008 Paris
Tel.: 01-40-07-72-50
Web: http://www.bel-group.com/

Marie-Anne Cantin
Address: 12, rue du Champ-de-Mars,
75007 Paris
Tel.: 01-45-50-43-94
Email: contact@cantin.fr
Web: http://www.cantin.fr/

Maubert-Mutualité
Crémerie Quatrehomme, La Maison du
Fromage
118, rue Mouffetard, 75005 Paris

Rouge Crème
46, rue Madame, 75006 Paris
Tel.: 01-45-44-11-00, St-Sulpice

Rue du Bac
Christian Guillot, De L'Entrée au Dessert
Address: 45, rue de Babylone, 75007 Paris
Tel.: 01-47-05-85-00, St-François Xavier

Rue du Bac, Solférino
Fromagerie Barthélémy (Sté)
Address: 51, rue de Grenelle, 75007 Paris
Tel.: 01-42-22-82-24, 01-45-48-56-75

S.E.L.L., La Ferme des Arènes
60, rue Monge, 75005 Paris
Tel.: 01-43-36-07-08, 01-43-36-37-38

Appendix C. Conversion Tables

Temperature Conversions

Gas mark	Fahrenheit	Celsius	Descriptive
¼	225°	107°	Very Slow/Very Low
½	250°	121°	Very Slow/Very Low
1	275°	135°	Slow/Low
2	300°	149°	Slow/Low
3	325°	163°	Moderately Slow/Warm
4	350°	177°	Moderate/Medium
5	375°	191°	Moderate/Moderately Hot
6	400°	204°	Moderately Hot
7	425°	218°	Hot
8	450°	232°	Hot/Very Hot
9	475°	246°	Very Hot

Weight-to-Volume Conversions

Dry Ingredients
1 pound flour = 4 cups
0.5 ounce flour = 1 level tablespoon
1 ounce flour = 1 heaped tablespoon
1 pound granulated sugar = 2 cups
1 ounce granulated sugar = 1 tablespoon
1 pound caster/superfine sugar = 2 cups
1 ounce caster/superfine sugar = 1 tablespoon
1 pound icing/confectioner's sugar = 3 cups
1 ounce icing/confectioner's sugar = 1½ tablespoons
1 pound brown sugar = 2½ cups
1 pound dried fruit = 2 cups
1 pound fine, dry bread crumbs = 4 cups
2 ounces fresh bread crumbs = 1 cup
6 ounces slivered almonds = 1½ cups
4 ounces ground almonds - 1 cup
3.5 ounces rolled oats = 1 cup
1 ounce nuts (whole, shelled) = ¼ cup

Fats, Lards and Solid Oils
1 pound butter or lard = 2 cups
0.5 ounce butter = 1 tablespoon

Beans and Rice
1 pound rice = 2 cups
1 pound dried beans = 2 cups

Meats and Cheese
1 pound chopped meat = 2 cups
2 ounces shredded cheese = ½ cup

Appendix D.
The Great Wheel of the Year Association Chart

It would be short-sighted to recognize only a few ancient holidays as the primary source for all modern-day Paganus events, just as it would be unfair to exclude even the most mundane or esoteric celebration due to its extinction in the lexicon of current cultural occurrences. Indeed, there are literally hundreds of holidays to recognize in one season; each season would constitute an entire book. And there are an astounding number of ways in which winter and mid-winter solstices alone are observed.

There are as many observances as there are people on the earth. In ancient Greece, there was the *Brumalia* festival, whereas the Roman Empire celebrated *Saturnalia* and *Dies Natalis Solis Invicti*. The ancient Gauls honored *Deuorius Riuri* and in East Asia and ancient Japan, *Amaterasu*, *Dōngzhì* and *Tōji* served as a yearly winter celebration. For the ancient Zoroastrians, there was *Deygān* and *Maidyarem*, while the ancient Persians had *Yalda*, and the Kurds Şeva *Zistanê*. The ancient Buddhists of Sri Lanka had *Sanghamitta Day*, and Indian Hindus enjoyed the *Lohri*, *Pongal*, and the *Makar–Sankranti* festivals. The list continues with *Midvinterblót* for the Swedes and many Norse peoples, and *Mōdraniht* for many of Western Germany. While there was *Hogmanay* in Scotland, many ancient Celts observed the Montol Festival and Mummer's Day, as well as Wren's Day. Even in the South American cultures of Peru, Bolivia, and Ecuador, there was *Inti Raymi* and *We Tripantu* to honor the winter solstices and its significance of life, growth, and death of the seasons. And there are many, many more.

Although the *Great Wheel of the Year* is largely a contemporary invention formulated by several orders during the mid-twentieth century—specifically from the New Forest Coven and from Gerald Gardener's Hertfordshire coven known as the Bricket Wood Coven in Hertfordshire, England, it continues to serve many modern-day Paganus folk. Likewise, other orders and individuals have contributed ancient ideas about how the solar cycles and equinoxes functioned, thus creating the various seasons and their attributes in the process. Gerald Gardener and his contemporaries, such as Alex Sanders, Dayonis, Doreen Valiente, Egyptologist Margaret Murray, and even famed psychologist Carl Jung, have all contributed to this fledgling concept. Indeed, it was during this time when the popular holiday names of Halloween, Candlemas, Beltane, and Lammas were officially formed. Later, other additions such as *Litha* and *Mabon* would be added by occult scholar Aidan Kelly to highlight possible ritual customs for minor solstices and equinoxes by ancient peoples. All happily being utilized and enjoyed to this day.

Most historians agree that these holidays are based on ancient customs founded in Europe, particularly within the Pan-Celtic, Scandinavian, and Germanic traditions. Today, modern Paganus peoples celebrate eight major seasonal holidays and cross-quarter days, though there are also various minor observances such as *Vali's Blot* on February 14, serving as a Valentine's-like celebration honoring the god Váli, or *Yggdrasil Day*, which celebrates tree and nature rites from Norse and Germanic history on April 22. Other minor holidays like *Summerfinding*, which recognizes the beginning of summer, resting between Ôstara and *Walpurgis Night* around April 13–20 are also common, as is the celebration of *Winterfinding*, observed around late September to mid-October, denoting the true beginning of winter for many Norse and Germanic paths. Needless to say, Paganus peoples, both ancient and contemporary have much to be proud of. The individual names and customs attached to such seasonal charts are also many, though there is a simple manner in which to view each season and its method, so I will use the most common here to best represent the colors, scents, and aesthetics, as well as the proper foods and libations that will best denote our ancestors' way of life. Though these tables will exemplify a common link between Christian and Paganus peoples of an ancient age, they should be observed as you see fit.

Below are some possibilities for holidays and celebrations, which can be altered and added to with colors and handmade aesthetics to praise a certain path, or made simple with only the bare essentials. There are also suggestions on food and drink ideas to best denote the event. Note that these are my personal picks; I have experienced some of the music, for instance, while working with groups and societies; other music is from my own collections. Whatever the spirit yearns for, it must be for you, so experiment and enjoy— These are your holidays!

Samhain (Paganus New Year—The Third Harvest)

Samhain (pronounced sow-een), is honored on October 31 (on April 30 in the Southern Hemisphere) and serves as a juncture for the winter solstice and as the New Year for modern pagans. In ancient Celtic cultures, this season represented the great fire festivals, where Paganus folk would light fires throughout the countryside to brighten the darkest time of the year and show respect for the fallen god. The ancients believed that a god had died. Though the wife, the goddess, would mourn the loss, she was also grateful, for she carried within her a new god yet to be born. These were simple ways of explaining the dark seasons and the return of the summer, for which the old lands waited eagerly. This holiday, the New Year, is a time for renewal of one's spirit. It is a time for putting away doubt and conquering personal weaknesses. It is a time of great celebration for a new year ahead and hope for a joyous and prosperous year for family and friends.

Colors and aesthetics: black, orange, and white
Use these colors to represent the darkness of the night, the shadows that lie over the land, and the glow of ancient fires that once lit the skies. White represents hope for the year ahead and the promise you'll make in secret. Use a selection of candles, tablecloths, or altar covers in these colors.

Trees, fruits and herbs: apples, pumpkins, turnips, gourds, mistletoe, and willow trees
Seasonal fruit trees, such as apple trees, represented a source of food and drink for the ancients, as did vegetables such as turnips, which were hollowed out to hold a candle to light the path for spirits returning to the living on this sacred night. Though pumpkins weren't introduced to the colonists until much later in history, be sure to light a variety of these ancient icons to honor the departed. The ancients would use boughs of willow and mistletoe to adorn tables and altars, and were sure to have plenty of the seasonal fruit to serve as an offering, both in remembrance and for the health and benefit of family and friends.

Animal icons: bats, cats, ravens, spiders, and wolves
Like the creatures expected to be found in the season of All Hallows' Eve, these animals and insects represent the things that creep by night and fly when the moon is full. Though simply natural things of the earth, they take on a frightening effect for those who do not respect such parts of nature. For Paganus folk, however, both old and new, they represent

an important aspect of nature and the dark side that resides within us all. The ancients would decorate with effigies or dead specimens of these creatures as a sign of respect, as did ancient ceremonial magicians who believed that the spirit of these creatures would aid in their magic. You may use aspects of these animals, such as a wolf pelt or bat wing, as did the ancients, or simply use effigies and other likenesses to add to the natural feeling this holiday inspires.

Scents and music: apples, oranges, and burning wood, classical music
To enhance the feeling of this holiday, try to recreate a relaxing and exotic foundation for your activities. There is a bit of psychology here, and if done properly, the festive smells, colors, and music will be remembered for many years to come. For scents, bubbling apples mixed with spices such as clove, nutmeg, and cinnamon add to the mystery of the holiday. So does the burning of resins, like Copal and Dragon's Blood, as well as powdered clove, which will ground the area and make the air smell exotically pleasant. For music, a lively selection of tunes will work, such as from the Australian group Dead Can Dance, performed by Lisa Gerrard and Brendan Perry. When the mood settles, consider the quintessentially somber notes of Hector Berliounce and Béla Bartók; both are able to evoke the mood of impending snow, thus creating a subtle foreboding the ancients would have felt. It also creates a bit of a chill too, but in a delightful way.

Foods and libations: Spicy drinks, nuts, sauced meats, and seasonal vegetables
Because this season was a time of celebration and a way to harness the fear of the coming winter, fruits and nuts associated with the winter months are always best. Walnuts, chestnuts, apples, and berries are good starters and can be served in bowls around the house. They warms the area and offer a chance for friends and family to snack and mingle before the meal. With this, serve a variety of seasonal beers and wines. For a non-alcoholic beverage, offer apple cider. For those with adult tastes, consider Cock Ale, Raisin Stepony Wine, and Metheglin Cornish Ginger Wine. When ready to serve food, you may wish to offer several loaves of bread, such as Manchet or Diar Bread, as well as light appetizers such as Funge (mushroom) Pasties and Pompys (Meatballs in sweet sauce). For the main meal, consider Welsh Roast of Pork or Roman-Anglo Roast of Lamb, and perhaps Rissoles Meat Tarts or Newtown Rabbit and Onion Pye. Because the ancients would often kill the weakest animals before the winter took hold, the feast could be quite elaborate. For sides, add bowls of Welsh Creamed Leeks, Roast Rosemary Potatoes and Onions in Cumin Sauce for a unique and hearty example of ancient Paganus hospitality. For dessert, offer Spice Bread or Medieval Apple and Pear Fritters to complete your journey into the past.

Be sure to offer a selection of after-dinner drinks such as a Brandy Syllabub or a flip to eloquently end the occasion. If possible, have a small fire burning in an outside fire pit. Alternately, gather a few candles to signify the fire and warmth of your community—the very essence of our ancestors.

Yule (Winter Solstice)

Celebrated between December 20 and 31 in the Northern Hemisphere and on June 21 in the Southern Hemisphere, Yule is a traditional holiday. Along with All Hallows' Eve and Easter, it is the most recognized world-wide, including by the Christian faith. As Samhain is synonymous with All Hallows' Eve, and Ôstara with Easter, Yule is synonymous with Christmas. The variations are actually quite small, though most Christians today are unaware of the history, to the chagrin of both scholars and contemporary pagans. The original Yule holiday celebrates the winter solstice, when the Holly King battles the Oak King for ruling rights. The Holly King wins and rules until midsummer. It is a time for slumber, waiting out the cold winds from the north, and a time for prayer and thanks for the food stored before the first frosts arrived, and for the bountiful harvest yet to come.

The ancients would have associated this holiday with the Wild Hunt and the Norse god Odin, in which the last hunting parties went out before the heavy snows set in. It is also associated with the pagan Anglo-Saxon rite known as *Modranicht*, meaning Mother's Night, where sacrifices were made on what is now known as Christmas Eve. Nonetheless, this is a time of fear—of the unknown and the darkness— but also joy in knowing that hope and trust will eventually come to pass. In short, this is a wonderful time, and should be praised to one's path, meaning that personal flair and enthusiasm should be seen by all who enter your home.

Colors and aesthetics: forest green, mulberry red, indigo blue and snow white
These basic colors represent nature and hold great significance for both the ancients and contemporary Paganus folk. Forest greens signify the very life that offered fruit and nuts, as well as a means for making shelter and defensive shields and weapons. Greens honors life and hope in many meaningful ways. Likewise, the color of mulberry; a deep, blood red also denotes the lifeblood of the trees and is a token of life offered to other living things, both man and animal. Blues and whites also have a place in this season, as they signify the darkness of the winter skies and the light of the stars and moon, offering a sense of hope for the coming midsummer. Add these accompanying colors to serving tables, altars, and your clothing to honor the season and inspire those around you.

Trees, fruits and herbs: apples, red currants, bayberry, mistletoe, and evergreen
There are two ways to symbolize steadfastness through the winter. The first signifies things that support life during the snowy winter, such as apples and berries. The second concept is the hearty greens that do not fade in the bitter cold. The bayberry, holly, and evergreen remain thick and fragrant no matter how frigid the winds blow, as does the mistletoe, which hibernates at the tops of trees. Offer bowls of pinecones to signify sturdiness and self-esteem, put up boughs of bayberry leaves mixed with branches of evergreen, tied with ribbons of corresponding colors, to greet friends old and new and ensure that old things pass and new things will come.

Animal icons: The stag, snow fox, boar, bear, and dove
The deer, stag, bear, and boar have direct lineages to the ancient Celts, Britons, and Anglo-Saxons. They represent strength and longevity, the ability to survive almost any adversary, whether nature or a predator. The dove and snow fox represent speed and agility—the ability to "outrun" the sleet and snow. The ancients understood the path of nature and that which flourishes, so be sure to honor these stout and quick icons of old with natural effigies of these creatures, such as the antlers of a stag or claws of a bear. You can show reverence through creative designs on foods as well. When making meat or fruit pies, pay homage to the animal that represents your spirit or your group by adding a dough representation on the top. Doing so not only honors the ancients, but also livens-up the appearance of foods.

Scents and music: frankincense, myrrh, and acacia gum; classical quartets
Believe it or not, frankincense and myrrh were resin incenses cherished by magi centuries before the wise men offered them as gifts to the Christ child. Indeed, Chinese magi and

physicians used them almost 500 years before the birth of Jesus. Not only this, but scholars now believe that the gummy sap that oozes from the *Boswellia* and *Commiphora trees* native to Asia, Africa, and various parts of the Middle East may have many healing properties for aches and pains, arthritis, and even headaches. Magically, of course, both have properties that repel negativity and evil influences, which may be the reason so many Christian churches continue to use the smoke in their rituals. Either way, ancient Paganus folk were no different, as they also prized the rare resin for its supernatural forces.

When celebrating yuletide and the winter solstice, be sure to burn the delightful resin of frankincense and myrrh for an uplifting and spiritual feeling so synonymous with the season. Add a few grains of acacia gum resin for an exotic scent. Bayberry candles are also appropriate; they ground the area with the aroma that has enticed our ancestors for centuries.

When selecting music for the yule holiday, notably that which goes beyond the commercial spectrum, we might be hard-pressed to find just the right music to fit the mood of modern-day Paganus folk. Yet, with a little searching, you'll be surprised just how much is out there. When I celebrate with friends, where food and drink is abundant, I tend to have Celtic folk music playing; such as Enya or Clannad. Artists like Lisa Thiel, Dar Williams, Emerald Rose, and Loreena McKennitt are also wonderful examples of bright and positive music that will settle and inspire. These artists are viewed as true icons of the Paganus path. When sitting for the main meal, I find that soft, sophisticated music such as chamber music and classical quartets are perfect for settling the soul and grounding the area. The right music makes all the difference in the world.

Foods and libations: wassail, Chawetty tarts, heavy meats, and assorted side dishes
Whether it was called *Wæs þu hæl*, (which translates be thou hail) by the ancient Anglo-Saxons, or *Ves heill* by the ancient Norseman, the curious act of wassailing was an ode and a gift back to nature. Though thought of as a Victorian-era custom, where nicely dressed men and women walked the city streets caroling or collecting money for the poor, it was a celebration of life and a commemoration of the apple tree harvest. It was not uncommon for villagers to take to the orchards with spiced-apple drink and loaves of bread. They would soak up the drink with pieces of bread and then squeeze the liquid into the cracks of the trees to offer thanks for a bountiful orchard and a plea for another good harvest.

When celebrating the yuletide season, you might want to begin with Yuletide Wassail, the highly festive and spiced drink of history. Other drinks to accompany this could be Hippocras, also called Tripple, and Hogmanay Berry Bounce. Each is a customary beverage and can be used for opening yule rituals and served with meals. Consider natural berry teas and drinks, as well as apple cider, for those who wish to abstain from alcohol. For starters, offer bowls of assorted nuts and seasonal fruits, such as apples, blackberries, red currants, blueberries, and some types of winterberries. For the main meal, begin with Parsley, Onion, and Sage Salade and a selection of hot soups, such as Bosham Lobster Soup, Stewed Pompion (a spicy pumpkin soup), and Pease Pottage with toasted bread wedges.

For the feast itself, consider dishes like Roasted Honey Chicken, which always gets compliments. Offer sweet and spicy Chawetty Tarts, time-honored meat pie that goes along with the yule season as much as a warm cup of Wassail, and perhaps Dr. Dee's Roast Beef and Crisps, an English delight from Elizabethan times. Other meats like Cavalier's Venison Pottage and Cornish sausages, along with side dishes like Scotch Clapshot Potatoes, Frumenty (a thick wheat stuffing), and Onions in Cumin Sauce are great choices for a celebratory meal of great regard. For dessert, consider traditional Cornish Figgie Hobbin and Clotted Cream and English Syllabub, along with a plate of candied fruit to round out your event.

After-dinner drinks such Brandy Syllabub or Raspberry Shrub are excellent choices for this holiday, as the spicy, fruity tastes will unite a sense of the ancient with a warm feeling among. Light a fire pit or gather a few candles to signify the fire and warmth of your community and the very life of our ancestors.

Imbolc (Festival of Lights)

Imbolc (pronounced (em-bulk), celebrated on February 2 and 4, and on August 1 in the Southern Hemisphere, was known to the ancient Celts as *Oimelc*, translating to "milk of the ewe." This time of year is midway to spring. Change is coming; the sun is brighter and the land just a bit warmer. As the mother bird feeds her young and birds warn that spring is near, it is time to prepare. For many Paganus peoples, it signifies the maiden aspect of the triad, the young lady preparing for womanhood. The ancient Celts gave great devotion to the feminine and birthing aspects of this holiday, especially within the history of Brighid—Goddess of the British Isles. She was worshipped throughout the land until Christianity arrived. However, the goddess persona was difficult to quell, so she was conveniently demoted to the category of saint, thus becoming Saint Brighid of Kildare (c. 451 to 523 CE). She remains a Pagan icon as one of the Celtic "triune" goddesses, meaning that she is one and three simultaneously—maiden, mother, and crone. Imbolc as a Greater Sabbat is known by various names; the Teutonic path calls it Disting, and is observed February 14, while the Strega refer to it as Lupercus. And then there's Candlelaria in Mexico, and other events such as the Festival of Lights and the Snowdrop Festival.

Imbolc is a time of great joy and of preparation—joy, that the winter is showing signs of change, and preparation for cleaning home and hearth. Now is a good time to begin cleaning and getting ready, as the year is still just beginning. When celebrating in ancient times, wheat, barley, and cornhusk poppets, which adorned brides' clothing, were made to honor the pure goddess and bless the crops. The ancients would have also lit colorful candles to denote the many colors of the flowers and the rainbows brought on by the cleansing rains. As the colorful candles represent the many colors of the spring, they act as a magnet, gently nudging nature to bring these bright and beautiful tendrils of the earth back to us again, and soon. It was also a time for dance, poetry reading, and honoring the maiden spirit of humankind. This is a time to hear the odes of nature, the crying of babies, and the singing of birds; it is a time to rejoice and give thanks, but most of all, to know that to each season there is a beginning, middle, end, and a beginning once again.

Colors and aesthetics: white, rich green, and bright red
Though many colors are associated with Imbolc, three basic colors traditionally denote Brighid, the ancient goddess of the British Isles. Bright green symbolizes the mantle and cloak she wore, white the newly driven snow, and red the rising sun. Other colors such as pinks, yellows, blues, violets, and reds signify the bountiful spectrum of spring flowers. Add these colors to your candle selections as a way to honor the winter and the sleep it represents, as well as the coming spring and the awaking of nature.

Trees, fruits and herbs: angelica, basil, blackberries, celandine, heather and violets
To honor the goddess Brighid, dress your tables or altars with the bright green of spring that she favored. Some enjoy offering swaths of colorful garments as a gesture, leaving them

outside your door before retiring to bed. According to one legend, the maiden bestows blessing on a home and family for the offering; others believe it to be a sacrament. Either way, the action is a time-honored one, and shows respect and honor. In some traditions, this is a time to offer plates of berries and seasonal fruits and flowers of every kind. Consider scattering heather and violets about the altar, with boughs of pine wrapped in purple cloth. Light nature-colored candles as you and your friends pray for a healthy and happy spring.

Animal icons: sheep, ewes, lambs, and cattle
As this season is an ode to life and the birth of new life, consider the pelts of sheep and lamb as a testament to growth and longevity. Many have used such pelts as a cowl over robes and ceremonial vestments; others wear bright, colorful clothing.

Scents and music: floral and amber; Blackmore's Night and Eliseo Mauas Pinto
If there's one description for the scent of Imbolc and the quest for springtime, it has to be that of flowers. As Imbolc represents the brightness of spring, clean air, and fresh beginnings, I like to make sure the air is not too clouded or heavy when I celebrate. To that end, I choose essential oils over resins or powdered incense, which produces heavy smoke. I burn oils over a tea light burner. This creates a soft, yet elegant scent that will fill your home or sacred place evenly and ground the area nicely. With floral scents such as rose, helichrysum, and honeysuckle, you'll feel a gentle connection with nature, just as cedarwood, sandalwood, lavender, rosemary, and clove will suggest all the elements of a sacred presence.

Music should fill the air just as eloquently. I prefer lively tunes rather than overly contemplative lyrics. Imagine a young, fire-haired Brighid walking soulfully through the ancient woodlands, enjoying nature, sharing her innocence with the world. To match this image I would choose the lively works of Blackmore's Night, a British and American folk rock group formed by Ritchie Blackmore and Candice Night. Their heart and soul is not only heard, but emotionally felt. In addition, the works of Eliseo Mauas Pinto on harp, guitar, and other instruments are traditional and deep in meaning.

Foods and libations: Stepony wine, warm breads, hot soups and assorted hors d'oeuvres
As this is a season that still has a cold bite, and as foods harvested earlier the year before are dwindling, Paganus peoples of old would have supped sparingly, making thick soups from barley and meal, as well as thin broths with eggs and dried herbs. These soups would have been poured into hollowed-out trencher breads and eaten with cheese and leftover meal for a hearty meal. Therefore, I suggest thick soups like the Elizabethan-era Pease Pottage, which is a thick split pea soup and will win the hearts of vegetarians everywhere, too. Another guaranteed favorite will be Crone's Four Bean Burgoo, an ultra thick mush-like bean stew that will fill you up and keep you warm no matter how cold it gets. Finally, I would suggest a genuine English Creamed Nut Soup, which is light, yet filling. For hors d'oeuvres, I like to serve authentic dishes that would have kept our ancestors alive during the long winters. Foods like Mortis de Chicken, a chicken pâté on toast, and Bacon and Egg Pye are delicious and simple to prepare. For the main meal, consider Welsh rarebit, also known as Caws Wedi Pobi, with a side of Welsh Creamed Leeks. A simple Spice Bread will end the celebration honorably.

After dinner drinks like Raisin Stepony Wine or a Ginger Wine are excellent choices for this holiday, as each offers a unique taste that will inspire any palate. For non-alcoholic drinks, serve black, green, and herbal teas and natural apple cider.

Ôstara (Spring Equinox)

Ôstara (oh-star-ah) is the season to be joyful and grateful and to clean house from top to bottom. Typically celebrated from March 10–23, and on September 21 in the Southern Hemisphere, this holiday signifies that spring has arrived and night and day are balanced once again. Flowers are blooming, birds are singing, and animals will soon be breeding. The maiden figure is still the focus, though this celebration originated in far earlier cultures than the Celtic traditions. Indeed, the ancient Egyptians observed the Festival of Isis, which denoted the age when the River Nile was rising, thus signifying the mournful tears shed by the goddess Isis for the fallen Osiris. Both ancient and modern-day Jews celebrate Passover in observance of the great exodus from Egypt and years of indentured slavery. To this day, the festivities are joyous; homes are cleaned throughout, stories are told, and Seder feasts are held. The Christians have Easter, representing the ascension of Christ after the crucifixion. Chocolate bunnies and lambs and colorful jellybeans, as well as the traditional "spring cleaning" symbolize a reverence for fertility and rebirth. There are literally hundreds of rituals and celebrations honoring spring throughout ancient times to the present, yet are these holidays really different from each other?

Easter originated from the German word Ostern, later known as Eostre and Eastre among Anglo-Saxon Paganus folk. The term actually refers to the ancient goddess of the same name. This jovial goddess would bring joy and life to humanity each spring as the Sun King departed across the skies. She arrived with a magical rabbit who would breathe new life into the plants and ground. She also carried a basket filled with bright, colorful eggs, which she hid behind the new blades of grass for people to find as a gift of new life. Does this sound remotely familiar? Indeed, it might surprise us to realize just how connected we humans actually are.

Whatever your personal affiliation, express Ôstara in the gayest way possible. It is a time for celebrating new life and a chance to make amends to the earth and all humankind by planting new seeds and tilling the ground. Serve your community with foods and libations, song and dance—and yes, having an egg hunt too!

Colors and aesthetics: gold, light greens, and pastel colors of every tint and hue.
As Christians honor Jesus' rebirth into uncorrupted perfection, the Paganus peoples recognized the continuation of life on earth with festive, yet calming colors of shadowed purples and saffron yellows, light greens, pinkish reds, and somber blues. The goddess Ôstara laid the eggs, representing the "world egg" that was then given life from the Sun King's warmth, assuring prosperity and growth for the coming year. You, too, can follow these ancient, yet simple customs by dressing your home or sacred place with gold and light green candles to represent the golden warmth of the sun, and the light green for the new growth reaching through the melting snow. Use pastel colors to represent the many blooming flowers, and by all means offer colored hardboiled eggs and magical chocolate bunnies if you like. Above all, make your home a place of grand happiness, for you and I have been given a great gift.

Trees, fruits, and herbs: lilies, lavender, orrisroot, purple clover, violets and crocus
If you are setting up an altar or food table, consider a host of flowers and potted plants. Consider bright, highly scented flowers such as tansy, thyme, marjoram, tarragon, lovage, honeysuckle, daffodils, jonquil, and tulips. For fruits, offer apples, which would have been stored in cool barns and cellars for months. Serve rhubarb, stewed into a pottage or in a pie mixed with apples or ripe elderberries.

Animal icons: rabbits, chicks, the mistle thrush, and the fallow deer
Gentle and fertile creatures are the primary focus. The rabbit and the hare are known to be very fertile. The mistle thrush and the fallow deer are also creatures that will let us know that the snow is thawing, and that we can get back to nature where we belong. If it is not possible to honor this holiday with animals and birds, simply use photos or artistic renditions of our furry and feathered friends. This is a wonderful project for both young and old.

Scents and music: frankincense, myrrh, benzoin, and lavender resins, Maggie Sansone
Ôstara honors the feminine spirit and presence and the concepts of fertility and gratefulness. Although this season has its similarities to other faiths, its differences tend to honor nature and the return to nature more than anything else. Therefore, I suggest the sweet floral scent of lavender and the exotic essence of benzoin, mixed with the steadfast and powerful scents of frankincense and myrrh, to honor that the winter solstice has recently departed, and that the spring equinox has arrived. Used for sacred rites, protection, and purifying rituals, this resin mixture will fill the air with a delightful, yet spiritual feeling that all will enjoy. For music, the time-honored Scotch-Irish tunes of Maggie Sansone, Karen Ashbrook, and Robin Bullock are appropriate, as the historical sounds of hammered dulcimers, Irish flutes, and pipes are always bright and pleasant. The music will melt the heart just as the snow melts in spring, enticing even the rabbits to dance.

Foods and libations: Raspberry Shrub, watercress, spinach, honey chicken, and English biskets
Consider beginning with a tasty Raspberry Shrub, which you can make when the snow is still on the ground. This dark, sweet drink will give your guests a nice, warm glow as they arrive. Offer seasonal nuts, fruits such as berries and apples, and breads—classic English biskets are the best, especially when served warm with honey and spice butter. For the main meal, offer Roasted Honey Chicken, a truly sweet and robust meal that is as traditional as one can get. Also, consider serving Anglesey Eggs, a hot, cheesy potato and leek dish from ancient Wales, and Epinards à la Crème, a hearty French spinach soufflé that's a perfect example of spring foods of our Paganus ancestors. For dessert, think about serving authentic Elizabethan-era apple fritters, which would have been popular, as apples were nearing the end of their life after the long winter. As the fruit gets softer, they become perfect for frying. Offer a selection of candied fruits, too, which would have delighted everyone in an age before overly sweet chocolates and mass-produced treats were available.

After-dinner drinks like Raspberry Shrub and Raisin Stepony Wine are excellent choices for Ôstara, as each offers an authentic flavor. For a non-alcoholic drink, serve milk and honey, which would have been an ode to the nursing animals, and perhaps apple and berry herbal teas and natural apple ciders.

Beltane (Fertility Festival)
Beltane (pronounced bell-tain), celebrated between May 1 and May 4 in the Northern Hemisphere, and on October 31 in the Southern Hemisphere, represents a grand time of love and courtship for men and women, and a time for commitments and recommitments. Beltane, literally translating to the word May in Gaelic, and meaning "bright fire" within the Celtic context, consummates the pairing and mating ritual of the god and goddess, the lord and lady, and the passion of the ancient Paganus peoples. Whether celebrated as *Walpurgis Night* or *Walpurgisnacht* in Germany and Scandinavia, *Calan Haf* in Wales, *Lei Day* in the Hawaiian Islands, *Arminden* in Romania, or *Fiesta de las Cruces*, in Mexico

and Spain, the primary meaning remains the same. For many Roman Catholics, May Day is symbolized by Mary's Month, in which the Blessed Virgin Mary is seen wearing a crown of flowers celebrating god and goddess, man and wife, and birth.

For the ancient Celts, Beltane brought great fire festivals in praise of deities that represented fire and passion, such as Pan, Belenos, and Eros, as well as female counterparts Astarte, Maia, Flora, and Freyja, and even the Green Man motif. It was and remains a time of recommiting marriages, handfastings, and sexual energies. Moreover, the maypole, its universal icon, is a consummate symbol representing the phallus, where the pole is the penis and the flowered wreath at its apex represents the vagina. Though the sexual elements are obvious, the emotional and spiritual aspects are equally potent.

Present-day Paganus folk continue to honor the holiday as a fertility rite by reenacting ancient customs, such as leaping over fires to secure a mate or as a plea for a healthy birth. This ancient ritual continues to be seen around the world. Likewise, bundled boughs of hawthorn and rowan, tied in colored cloth known as May boughs, are still hung over doorways to attract and admit love, or to deny and shun love, as had been done since the Middle Ages. What's more, it's the rite of fire, where massive bonfires were lit to honor the ancient gods and light the darkness, and dancing and song filled the air, mingling with the fiery lust that this season portrays.

Today, many of the Paganus paths create colorful woven baskets filled with flowers and sweets to offer as a gesture of this important Sabbat, dance merrily around maypoles tethered to colorful ribbons, and take part in handfasting ceremonies officiated by a high priest or priestess. It is a spiritual time that honors the importance of love and sex that creates life and shows faithfulness between a man and a woman. This is also a time to celebrate the earth, its ability to produce strong crops and healthy plants to eat, and to sustain animal life, which in turn sustains human life. It is a time for renewal and passion.

Colors and aesthetics: white, reds, and pink
Use these colors when offering odes of love to a mate or showing a gesture of faith to family and friends. Bundle your own boughs of herbs and flowers, using rowan twigs and hawthorn branches mixed with May tree blossoms. Wrap them in red cloth to denote love and attraction, pink for innocent love, and white for the betrothed. Add candles in these colors to your altar or food tables. Make your own May baskets by adding red, white, and pink ribbon swatches to woven wicker baskets, intermixed with seasonal flowers. Place eggs inside to signify fertility.

Trees, fruits, and herbs: roses, May blossoms, bluebells, cherries and assorted berries
As this holiday is best represented by the fertile earth and growth in general, choose a wide variety of flowers to adorn your tables. Whether in the home or a sacred place, add daisies and lilacs, primrose and angelica to baskets and bowls. Trees and plants are also appropriate: make miniature maypoles, ash twigs with tether strips of colorful cloth. Make your own wreaths of hawthorn, rowan, or pine, wrapped with the corresponding colors and interwoven with flowers to hang on your door or offer as gifts. For snacks, offer bowls of seasonal nuts and hearty, dark red fruits like cherries, blueberries, and strawberries as a symbol of love and lust.

Animal icons: hares, goats, and honey bees
The ancient Paganus peoples of the Celtic and Germanic paths would have given great respect to the fantastic creatures of lore, such as faeries, satyrs, giants, and many a winged creature.

Yet, there were many other creatures from the mundane world—such as rabbits, hares, goats, pheasants, and the honey bee—that nest and carry seed to spawn new life. In honoring them, we acknowledge their natural desire to procreate and keep the lines going. Life was precious to our ancient ancestors, as many might not reach adulthood due to disease, famine, or war. There was fear that a crop would not grow or that livestock might perish during the cold winters. In mirroring this custom, share effigies of these animals or offer items associated with them as your decorations. Honey wines and meads are often served at Beltane events and fire festivals, as well as greens and leafy salads, which are the primary foods of the propagating rabbit and hare, as well as the horned goat. Therefore, offering simple to exotic salads will show your knowledge and understanding of the old ways.

Scents and music: patchouli, jasmine, cinnamon, and dragon's blood; folk music
The scent that denotes the firefly passion of lust and love should honor the presence of woman and man, lord and lady. I have found that the earthy scents of patchouli and jasmine truly represent the female spirit, as dragon's blood does the male spirit. When a touch of cinnamon is added, the mixture becomes something quite exotic, drawing memories of the ancient north of long ago. Simply use the essential oils of these scents in an oil censor by adding five drops of each liquid. If you can't find the proper essential oils, or if they are too expensive, you can substitute synthetic oils.

For music, the undiluted sounds of independent folk artists fit the mood of Beltane. One of my favorite groups is Mysteria, a folksy metal group from Finland with Gothic overtones. Their music will appeal to the younger crowd nicely. Other independent artists like Catherine Lambert and Kellianna are great examples of song and chant inspired by myth, magic, and sacred places. The gentle mixing of guitar and vocals, chants and esoteric sounds will bring life to your events and holidays, honoring the sagas of the gods and goddesses of the old religions.

Foods and libations: Metheglin, Welsh Cakes, Folk Herb Salat, and Cawl Cymreig
As this holiday honors life and procreation of all living things, it seems logical to honor those creations equally. I like to start off with the nectar from the flowers after it was courted by the honey bees, giving us the thick, sweet goodness of honey. Metheglin Ginger Mead is an excellent sweet, crisp beverage that will open your event or ceremony splendidly. With this, I offer plates of spicy Welsh Cakes, similar to a traditional crumpet. This sweet bread goes exceedingly well with ginger mead. I like to make mine with red currants or edible winterberries, though blueberries work well, too. Next, because roughage of all sorts is appropriate, I will often serve a selection of greens, such as an Herb Salat, Watercress and Violet Salat, or a Parsley, Onion, and Sage Salade. Each is hearty enough to be a meal and also looks great on the table. After the salad, I traditionally offer authentic Cawl, a thick Welsh stew, and Carotea et Pastinacas, which are sautéed carrots and parsnips, served hot. Make plenty, as it usually goes fast. For dessert, I might serve Almond Ryce, a simple almond rice pudding served in sundae glasses. Offered chilled or warm, topped with nutmeg, and accompanied with a bowl of minced cherries or mulberries, it is a noble ending to the meal.

For an after-dinner drink, serve more of the Metheglin Ginger Wine, as it, too, is an excellent closing drink. The authentic spicy flavor and warmth of the ginger will settle the stomach and please the palate. For non-alcoholic drinks, serve whole, organic milk, which would have been an ode for the nursing babies, both human and animal. Offer a selection of herbal teas as you reminisce with your loved ones.

Litha (Midsummer Solstice)

Litha, also known as Midsummer Solstice, is celebrated between June 20 and 23 in the Northern Hemisphere, and on December 21 in the Southern Hemisphere. It is the polar opposite of Yule in the Great Wheel of the Year—a time of the Sun King's most powerful reign in the sky and the longest day of sun. It is also a time for the fullest greens and ripe fruits and vegetables to jut from the earth in all their glory.

The concept of Litha is still vague to many scholars, though it is believed to have been a form of ancient ritual Aerra Litha, meaning the month of June during the time of the Saxon barbarian migrations, around the fifth to seventh centuries. During this time many Ingaevones tribes, also known as the Oceanus Germanicus, or the People of Yngvi by the Romans, were settling in ancient Britannia. These Germanic peoples were able to appreciate the green forests and grassy valleys, intermingling their folk beliefs and traditions with that of Anglo Paganus folk, and forming many of the customs we see today. In 1973 occult scholar Aidan A. Kelly formulated the modern concept for the holidays of Litha and Mabon. Because there were no official pagan names to honor the summer solstice and autumn equinox equivalent to Ôstara and Beltane, he studied many texts, both ancient and contemporary, to find a logical solution. By examining ancient sources, such as the Saxon calendar, which was described by the English scholar known as Bede the Venerable, (672–735), he found logical names for these two respectable holidays, which remain in the conscious of modern Paganus folk everywhere.

Jack-in-the-Green, or the Green Man, for instance, is one of the most recognized images of summer. It represents the green and leafy life that intermingles with the human spirit, creating a hybrid of all things in life, and which is steadfast throughout. As the ancients would have honored the green life around them, they would have also understood the importance of fire and water and the heat and cold, which was observed in the skies when the thunder boomed and the rain fell on the crops. Indeed, they would set great bonfires blazing on the mountains to show their devotion and have joyous gatherings with green foods and breads. They would dress as the mysterious Green Man with masks made from oak leaves and ivy, wearing shafts of grain and roots, and dancing about in laughter and song. They would set wagon wheels afire and roll them into lakes and ponds to appease and praise the Sun King.

Now is the time to take full advantage of the gifts of the Green Man—the extra hours of daylight to work in your gardens and to run happy and free under the warm sun. Simple things for us today, they were grand gifts to be honored by our northern ancestors, who were practically held hostage by the powerful winds and bitter cold. Though the solar festivals were added later in history, likely as a result of travel though the Middle East and Asia, there is evidence that ancient Europeans noted the importance of this aspect of the Great Wheel of the Year. The sheer mystery of this season, and its simple idea, makes it worth honoring today.

Colors and aesthetics: greens, golden-yellows, and maroons

The focus is on greens for the living earth, golden-yellows for the blazing sun at midday, and hazy gold and amber hues for the summer evenings. Maroon and similar reds stand for the berries, apples, and bonfires that this holiday signifies. Place colorful candles on oak leaves around the house and in sacred places. Serve bowls of nuts and red fruits, oats and grains, and pitchers of milk and honey as offerings to all that gives us life. Take it a step further with a blazing fire pit where you gather, and offer pieces of oak to the fire as thanks for the season. Wear loose-fitting cloths in these warm colors and show your reverence by singing and dancing as our ancient ancestors did centuries ago.

Trees, fruits, and herbs: oak, mugwort, chamomile, honeysuckle, ivy, and berries
In terms of wood, this Sabbat holiday is best represented by the mighty oak, which made the sturdiest dwellings in ancient times, other than stone. It also formed the strongest shields for combat and was the choice armor for the mighty ships that dominated the seas. In addition to this, fir trees, ferns, and herbs such as mint, basil, parsley, and thyme represent the mid-summer woods. Ivy, known as *gort* to the ancient Celts, was seen as the canvas that wove life wherever it crawled, just as honeysuckle's signature scent denotes the breath of nature gently sighing over all things. Use these herbs and portions of these bushes and trees to decorate your home. Make boughs of fir and other hearty pines and their cones to line your serving tables and altars, and wrap candles with the dark green ivy leaves. Keep plenty of fresh flowers and vegetables on hand, too, as well as bowls of ripe blackberries, blueberries, and strawberries, as the garden was one of the key features of Paganus peoples everywhere.

Animal icons: robins, wrens, horses, satyrs, faeries, and the Green Man
As summer arrives, we see birds and animals making their home in the trees, burrowing holes for their families, and gathering seeds, nuts, and berries for their own celebrations. Horses and livestock run and play, and the hidden creatures of myth hide and frolic through the woodlands. The cloven feet of Pan and other satyrs can be heard trotting in the thickets, jack-in-the-green can be seen peering through the leaves of the berry bushes, and even the dragons are lying lazily on the banks of lakes enjoying the warm sun—ask any child. This is a time for loud and exultant celebrations, with backyard cookouts and families enjoying the pool or a game of horseshoes. Now is a good time to get involved with the kids and make masks of those fantastic creatures, such as the mischievous green man or a playful dragon, and construct frilly lace or paper faeries' wings. Play games of hide-and-seek in honor of the warm days and the quiet nights, and take full advantage of the warmth and light of this brilliant season.

Scents and music: cedar, pine and oak; Clannad
For lively, yet calming scents that best denote the summer of our ancestors, I have chosen the earthy scents of cedar, pine, and oak. Each essential oil or dry incense will fill the air with an earthy scent reminiscent of a faraway land. When the doors are open, and when the gentle summer breeze flows through, the mixture of these woodsy bouquets will honor this solstice evenly and appropriately. The singular scents of heliotrope, oranges, wisteria, frankincense, myrrh, cinnamon, sandalwood, and clove work well, too. For a nice, spicy scent that will fill the air like none other, I like to put a few pinches of powdered clove in a metal bowl or hanging censer and light it. It will burn down naturally and give off a pure smoke that grounds and sanctifies, much like frankincense and myrrh. Oils and scented waxes melted over tea lights are always good in the home, and because there are so many summer-like fragrances available, you'll have an almost limitless selection to choose from. For music that's full of life and thoroughly enjoyable on so many levels, try Clannad for Litha celebrations. A soulful mixture of folk, rock, ambient jazz, and world music, this family of musicians—Maire, Pol, and Ciaran Brennan—create modern, yet traditional tunes that will enliven and transfix. Their sister, Enya, is also a nice choice as the evening begins to fall.

Foods and libations: ale, diar bread, Salet of Lemmones, fish soup, and baked carp
Because Litha represents the sun and warmth; physical activity and the dance, we would favor lighter fare over heavy foods. To begin, serve light drinks like meads and wines or ales and flips. Offer bowls of popped corn, toasted grains, seasonal nuts, and deep red berries. Diar bread, a robust caraway meal bread, will prepare the palate for the main meal, though it is filling if served with the main meal. Offer honey butter with this, and be sure to have fresh vegetables, such as carrots, spring lettuce, spinach, and summer squash; and as fruits like oranges, quince, apples, and pineapples. When ready to eat, start with a Salet of Lemmones, thinly sliced, resting on leafy greens, and arranged on fancy plates. Next, offer an authentic Devonshire Fish Soup, a delightful combination of fish in a spicy broth, or perhaps Bosham Lobster Soup, which is thick and creamy, able to please even the most discerning taste. For the main meal, consider Baked Carp on a bed of kale with hardboiled eggs and sliced citrus. It's filling enough to satisfy even the most hungry, yet light enough that it won't slow you down. Add simple side dishes like Onions in Cumin Sauce and Roast Rosemary Potatoes. For dessert, offer a selection of candied fruits as a sweet, light finish to this special summer repast.

For an after-dinner drink, serve something that will balance the palate and calm the stomach, such as Cornish Ginger Wine or simple herbal teas, poured over ice. Add a few seasonal berries or orange slices to each glass for a refreshing and well-balanced end to a perfect Midsummer Solstice.

Lammas (The First Harvest)

Lammas, sometimes called Lambess, and often referred to as Lughnasadh (loo-naa-sah), is celebrated on August 1 or August 6, and on February 2 in the southern hemisphere. This holiday represents the harvest season, when the grains and corn are ready to be cut and baled. It is a time of great joy, as well as hope for the next harvest. The ancient Paganus people would have given great thanks to the goddess image, which has now transformed into the mother figure, as seen in the triad of life—the maiden child, mother, and crone. The mother aspect, known as Lammas, is seen as a sturdy, weathered woman, her hands callused and soiled from working in the fields, her face dark tan from days spent under the sun. She carries a basket filled with ripe fruits and vegetables, and sometimes a scything blade for harvesting. She smiles as a mother would smile at her children, for that is what Lammas represents—the life-giving mother.

In addition to Lammas, the ancient Celts also gave praise to Lugh, which would become "Lughnasadh" or "Samildanach" for many northern Paganus peoples. This god was known for his prowess as a skilled craftsman, creator of the spear and many tools of other trades. He was also skilled in the magickal arts, where divination and nature crafts were taught to men and women alike. He represents the masculine aspect of this holiday, and can be seen as a father figure, too. As such, the Lammas observance, also referred to as *hlaf-mas* meaning loaf-mass to the ancient Anglo-Saxons, was a time for festivals celebrating the wheat harvest and to appease the goddess for her kindness and love.

For present day Paganus folk of many paths, Lammas is positioned as a cross-quarter holiday between Litha, the summer solstice and Mabon, the autumn equinox, and recognizes that it won't be long until another long winter sets in. This holiday was, and continues to be, a time for crafts and the arts, with everyone getting involved. In addition to the art of cookery, which certainly figures into our ancient ancestors' way of life, there was also pottery-making, textiles, carpentry, and artisanship.

Embrace this important holiday by making creative things for your celebration, whether colorfully painted plates and bowls or woven boughs and wreaths of wheat and barley. How you express yourself is what counts.

In the tradition of Lammas, the Mother of the Harvest, and Lugh, the Long Arm of crafts and skills, consider making a few time-honored corn maidens, which date back to the stone age in ancient Greece, and can be seen in practically every culture on earth. These little dolls, or "poppet effigies," were made of corn husks, wheat, oat, rye, or barley. They were tied with string to form a body, often dressed with cloth, and offered as a sacrifice to the corn fields to secure favor from the god and goddess. This tradition continues to this day around the world.

Colors and aesthetics: reds, greens, golden-yellows, earth tones, bronze, and grays
This is a season of hot days and sultry nights and planting and watering crops, which is just as important today as it was centuries ago. Colors like bronze and saffron-yellows evoke swaying wheat fields and golden loaves of bread. In grays and reds we can see the thunderclouds that will water the crops, and the hue of the bonfires that lit up the wheat and cornfields to a color of blood, which equals life and longevity. Use these colors on tables and altars, in choosing blankets to rest on while enjoying the summer evenings, and in your apparel. For a nice touch of beauty, spread colorful dried leaves on your tables and add lots of green and saffron-colored candles to your table.

Trees, fruits, and herbs, and grains: wheat, cornstalks, barley, sunflower, and hollyhock
The holiday is devoted to the bounty of grains and the wonderful foods made from them. This is a season of robust gardens and golden fields, so be sure to add plenty of the herbs, plants, and grains to serving tables and sacred places. Consider adding to your table full-bodied herbs such as dill, yarrow, oats, rye, and corn, as well as seasonal fruits and nuts such as hazelnuts, chestnuts, walnuts, apples, lemons, and oranges. Dress bowls and altars with hazel and oak leaves, and drape grape vines over doorways to offer a feeling of life and sustenance, which was always on the minds of the ancient Paganus folk.

Animal icons: chickens, roosters, goats, milk cows, griffins, and basilisks
Just as grains and seeds were of prime importance ages ago, so too were the animals that were cared for during the winter months. The ancients gave due credit to cows and fowl for their gifts that helped make the loafs of bread and the milk and cheeses. Creatures of myth were honored, too. Fabulous winged griffins and those leathery serpents, the basilisks of folklore, would have filled many a story before the fire pit. Honor our ancestors' understanding of these beasts by creating effigies of them through art and foods, shaping breads to mimic these fantastic creatures, or molded with puddings and cakes, as was once done. Offer a pitcher of milk and bowls of honey along with many types of bread.

Scents and music: heather, sandalwood, and copal; Robin Bullock
For every season and holiday, there is a lexicon of scents to choose from. Heather is my favorite scent for First Harvest. Its rich purple flower was used to conjure friendly spirits and call for rain. Its scent is exotic, almost like an African violet, and will scent a room like that of some faraway temple. Although you may certainly burn the flowers whole as an offering, just as the ancients did, I suggest burning the essential oil over a tea candle for the best effect. This relatively inexpensive oil can be purchased in most new age or botanical shops. The resins or essential oils of sandalwood and copal are also appropriate, as is simply burning oak wood chips in a fire pit. For music, I have chosen the Celtic folk renditions of Robin Cook, an

excellent example of ancient music made for modern times. His talent on the guitar, Irish harp, cittern, and mandolin blends ancient melodies of the ancient Celts with that of their Appalachian descendants. His lively tunes create a seventeenth-century feeling.

Foods and libations: ales, Funge Pasties, Capons in Concy, and Apple and Pear Fritters
Much like Litha, the gleeful season of Lammas and the first harvest should offer a sense of gratefulness and an example of what the earth provides for us. It's always a good idea to share many loaves of breads, and even have some as departing gifts for your guests. Consider corn bread, barley cakes, and freshly baked squash muffins with honey butter. I also like to have several loafs of Trencher Meal bread and Manchet bread too. It's also appropriate to have a variety delicacies from nature, such as seasonal berries, apples, crabapples, and nuts, and ciders and ales made from the summer fruits and grains.

Set the tables with plates of Funge Pasties, sweet and spicy mushrooms and authentic Pompys, a medieval-style meatball dish served in a sweet sauce. Present platters of freshly made Coastal Crab Cakes bedded on kale or spinach leaves. For the main meal, consider the Medieval-era Capons in Concy, a delectable egg dish bound to make everyone happy. Serve this with bowls of hot Frumenty, a delicious wheat stuffing that's fit as a meal itself, and Scotch Clapshot potatoes, which is as unique as this season. Offer bowls of leek and garlic sauces, as well as slightly-warm herbal and honey butters for the many breads being served. Offer ale and cider throughout the meal, and when the meal is done, and if your guests are able to eat just one more item, consider Medieval Apple and Pear Fritters, served warm and dusted with a fine powdered sugar. In the end, you will have won favor with the ravished and finicky alike.

Be sure to offer a selection of after-dinner drinks like a Brandy Syllabub and natural ciders to eloquently end the occasion. Consider a glass of dark port wine or chilled herbal teas to settle the stomach. If possible, have a small fire pit available outside for burning oaks chips and for offering written prayers of gratitude and desire for a prosperous future.

Mabon (The Autumn Equinox—The Second Harvest)

Mabon (mah-bun) is observed between September 20 and 23 in the Northern Hemisphere and on March 21 in the Southern Hemisphere. This holiday represents a Paganus thanksgiving, where family and friends gather to give thanks and celebrate the second harvest. This was the time when the storage of foods for the winter made the crops and fields appear barren and almost lifeless. The trees were becoming bare, and the ground was layered with the greenish-gold leaves of the approaching fall. Our ancient ancestors realized how vital the harvests were and began marking that realization with a series of celebrations. It is a time for soulful grace, balance, and contemplation.

Although this holiday, like Litha, is not part of any known ancient Paganus custom or festival, it was likely modeled after the ancient September ritual of *haleg-monath*, meaning holy month. The occult scholar Aidan A. Kelly renamed the Autumnal Equinox festival Mabon in the early 1970s. Though this was part of an assignment for a course in religious studies, his idea caught on, and many modern pagans honor this equinox with his contributions. Regardless, the name Mabon is the name for the Welsh-Celtic god Mabon ap Modron or Maponos, which means the Great Son, according to "Kulwch and Olwen," a tale from the *Mabinogion*, an ancient collection of works compiled from the *Llyfr Coch Hergest*, the *Red Book of Hergest*, and the *Llyfr Gwyn Rhydderch*, the *White Book of Rhydderch*. Mabon was thought to have been human at one time and later elevated to a god-like figure. He was even reputed to have ridden with King Arthur during the Battle of Mons Badonicus, and was feared by the Romans as a great warrior and hunter. His stature represents strength and prowess, youth and skill; he is seen as the bearer of light and an icon for suffering and death, and for those who have been forgotten. Though the history is so fabulous that, in spite of there being so little literature about Mabon and his significance in the pantheon of Cymric and Gaulish gods, we can see Kelly's reason for highlighting this ancient god figure. Mabon served as a balance of light and darkness, just as this season does each year. And because the darkness will soon be dominating, we can see the third aspect of the goddess triad come into place. The crone, much like the descent of the seasons, signifies wisdom and experience, as the crops and fields have yielded their gifts faithfully and given life to the community. As the third and final harvest approaches for the year, we give our respects and honor to the fresh vegetables and ripe fruits and celebrate all that has been afforded us with praise and merriment.

Now is a good time to take a walk through nature, through the woods and places off the beaten path. Enjoy the remaining warmth and pay respects to the woodland animals. Pick fruit and gather nuts; harvest fresh herbs to make colorful wreaths and garlands for your home; prepare odes and offerings of thanks on parchment paper to be burned in fires, and give thanks for all you received this year. This is a time for family gatherings and to offer wisdom to the young, so rejoice loudly. Sing, dance, feast, and give praise for all that you have!

Colors and aesthetics: rust, orange, gold, violet, browns, and black
As golden-green leaves spiral to the ground, it's time to show the warmer hues of nature and the radiant flair of the fire, another source of life in ancient times. Use these warm colors in candles and in place settings and tablecloths, as well as in altar coverings and for banners. Decorate your home or sacred place with seasonal gourds and assorted squash and offer bowls of nuts and apples. You may wish to include vases of calendulas, passionflower, snapdragons, marigolds, or roses. Add dark earth-tones to your apparel. Though these colors may at first denote mourning, they only signal that a time of sleep is ahead. Prepare to rest, knowing that life shall return.

Trees, fruits and herbs: apples, grapes, sage, acorns, and thistle
As the weather begins to cool, and the harvest has been completed for the second time of the year, we might notice a feeling that time is running out, and that a much-needed sleep is coming. This is certainly so for nature, but also for the ancient Paganus folk, who would have baled the grain and put fruit to bushel, and prepared to conserve what they had because the ground would be frozen and game challenging to catch. This was a period of waste-not-want-not, which could mean feast or famine. Therefore, if a community had a lame animal that was not expected to survive the winter; it would be killed and prepared as a feast. If they had too much grain for their bins, they would barter for other foods, or simply make lots of bread and pies. So, the idea is to conserve, but eat hearty, too. Other plants and herbs associated with Mabon are fern, hazel, ivy, cedar wood, hops, barley, and acorns. For herbs there is Solomon's seal, milkweed, myrrh sap, oak leaves, pine cones, and sage. Offer these herbs displayed in bowls, or place around candles for a festive spirit, and offer these plants as parting gifts for friends and family. Doing so denotes that life is always waiting, that what appears to be death is simply a period of rest.

Animal icons: wolves, dogs, and the bird of prey; gnomes, elves, and the gulon
As our ancient ancestors prepared for the howling winds and frigid snow, they also

prepared for the hunt. The men used birds of prey and hunting dogs to round up animals for food, and the women and children gathered berries and nuts and apples in the orchards. They knew the importance of having a guardian and ally with them. As the hunting dogs and birds aided our ancestors in the hunt or the faithful dog watched over the women and children, they would have honored these companions by feeding them during the feast and playing with them. The wolf icon was also important for our ancestors, as they were hungry, too, often attacking livestock or people. So we honor them as the threat that made ancient life a challenge, but also for their prowess as astute hunters. From the realm of fantastic creatures, we see the sneaky, yet playful gnomes and elves of mirth and legend. There is also the ferocious gulon, a creature from the northern lands that resembled a gargoyle or chimera. Thought of as living in the mountains above the villages of old, these creatures figured in many Paganus legends. Now is a good time to pay tribute to these mythical creatures by having the children in your family create festive drawings and masks or add little effigies to tables and altars in praise and remembrance.

Scents and music: Arabian jasmine, sage, pine, and musk; Hesperus and Emer Kenny
When we think of a thanksgiving, we might think of the wafting scent of roasting game bird or baked ham. Though this would have been true, there would also have been cauldrons of smoldering flowers and herbs. The aromatic scent of Arabian jasmine flower brought back from the crusades would have been a coveted flower, and eventually was used as an essential oil or tincture in health and beauty products. Combine this essential oil with a few drops of musk oil to create a fragrance of long ago. In addition to this, consider the oils, powders, or resins of sage, clove, frankincense, myrrh, aloe woods, and cinnamon.

For music, I have selected the rare and historical tunes by Hesperus, an ensemble of musicians that play folk and early music. Made up of Tina Chancey and Scott Reiss, and formally the resident ensemble at the National Museum of American History, this group creates an authentic feel of the ancient by combining medieval and folk music. After the meal, when the sky begins to darken, I suggest playing the ethereal music of Emer Kenny, a relaxing blend of Celtic harp and gentle song that will sooth even the roughest soul. This Irish artist will create a calming atmosphere in which to contemplate the waning year and prosperous harvests ahead.

Foods and libations: Hippocras, Grete Pye, Codfish in Gravy, Vegetables and Syllabub
Now we begin to see the warm colors of the fall set into place. The trees are beginning to show signs of leaf departure and the apples hang low and ripe; the corn is full and ready to pick, and the wheat and barley had been reaped, leaving bare earth where full fields once stood. This is a time to reflect on what keeps us alive and healthy, and that the earth and sky are about to rest for a time. We must be prepared for that absence, as we store and hoard, but it's also a time to show our respect by feasting joyfully. Much like ripping the wrapping paper from a birthday gift, we celebrate gleefully. Begin by serving your guests chilled glasses of Cornish Ginger Wine or Metheglin Ginger Mead to warm and greet everyone. When ready to serve, offer fresh Parsley, Onion, and Sage Salade, a bold, leafy salad that will accompany warm Manchet bread. Next, consider serving bowls of English Creamed Nut Soup or Crème Almaundys and Herbe Broth with Eggs and Cheese, along with a plate of warm Winter Fest Squash muffins. This combination creates a meal all by itself, yet will happily create a sense of partaking in a tier-course meal, which was popular in ancient times. For the main meal, consider the traditional Grete Pye, which is filled with meats and sometimes vegetables and thick

gravy. They also make wonderful parting gifts in remembrance of the feast. In addition to this, think about serving a platter of Codfish in Gravy, bedded on kale or other leafy greens, to honor the sea. Serve several sides dishes, like corn, carrots, and potatoes. For dessert, offer Spicebrede and English Syllabub. The soft, spicy ginger bread is always best when accompanied with a rich, creamy Syllabub, where the spicy flavor and texture will make a delightful ending to a fabulous feast.

For an after-dinner drink, consider an authentic Hippocras served warm or at room temperature. As the spices and wine settle the stomach after a large meal, this ancient libation's purpose becomes clear. Offer hot herbal teas such as ginger or chamomile with honey for a non-alcoholic stomach relaxer.

And so ends this brief, yet detailed look into the various ways one can celebrate the ancient holidays. Whether for friends or family, or for large groups, consider the ideas listed here to enhance and liven your feasting experience that will last all your days. Just remember, the way you celebrate shows your knowledge of the ancient ways, but also your wisdom in that you're keeping the ancient path alive and well, with as much zeal as our ancestors had done centuries ago. Make merry and be glad!

A woodcut of Elizabethan clown William Kempe dancing a jig, ca. 1620. *Courtesy of Society for Creative Anachronism, Arts and Sciences of the Middle Ages and Renaissance*

Additional Music Selections

The following musicians, composers, and ensembles are a superb resource for period music that will accompany any event honorably. Because our ancestors would have enjoyed melodies that have a rare and exciting vibrancy that lifts the spirit and creates a deep-felt sense of contemplation, I feel these examples will create a bridge between the vast oceans of time and our present. One excellent example of this is the *St. George's Canzona*, as it's faithful to medieval and Renaissance tunes while using authentic instruments to create a festive atmosphere. This British-based orchestra, consort, and choir are likely one of the most honest innovators of medieval to new world music to date. Directed by John Sothcott, and compiled by Jon Stringer and Pierre F. Roberge, the following labels will help you create a fabulous recreation of an ancient feast or Renaissance banquet with knowledge and style.

Most of the better music stores and larger book retailers should be able to order these titles directly. And, of course, you may search the web for these and similar titles from various companies and clearinghouses. So, you will literally have hundreds, if not thousands, of selections devoted to ancient music to choose from.

Music of the Roundheads and Cavaliers (popular music c. 1630 to 1700). St. George's Canzona.

Courtly Pastimes of Sixteenth Century England (c. 1500 to 1580s). St. George's Canzona.

England Be Glad!—Patriotic and Heroic Songs from the Crusades to the Civil Wars (select music c. tenth century to seventeenth century). St. George's Canzona
A Tapestry of Music for King Charles I and his Cavaliers (popular and select music c. 1630s). St. George's Canzona.

A Tapestry of Music for Oliver Cromwell & His Roundheads (popular music c. 1640s). St. George's Canzona.

Merry It Is while Summer Lasts: A Collection of Medieval and Traditional Music from the Spring and Summer Festivals. St. George's Canzona.

Acknowledgments

From the conception of my research to its culmination, I had a great deal of assistance; otherwise I would not have been able to complete this intense journey into the culinary arts and rich lifestyles of our ancestors who dominated all classes and stations, from Christendom to the Paganus folk of Europe and abroad. I offer my veneration to the late Reverend Dr. Brian G. Turkington, a scholar and noble man who was far more than a mentor—a true friend who had a seemingly unending cache of knowledge. Thanks also to Dr. Barbara Dubois of Harvard University, Dr. James McAddams, and Dr. Aidan A. Kelly for their esoteric and folkloric knowledge and research assistance, and to my many colleagues and friends who offered their time and efforts.

I also wish to acknowledge the research of Margaret "Maggie" Black (1921–1999) into her country's ancient cooking techniques, and to thank the British Library for its assistance and nearly inexhaustible collection of ancient documents. Thank you to the Bibliothèque Nationale de France, specifically the private collections department, without which this project could not faithfully be rendered.

I am grateful to the University of Southern California Library and the University of Chicago Library for their contributions, to my former professors at Norwich University for their assistance, and to those true authorities of history, anthropology, and ancient customs: Gerald Brosseau Gardner, Margaret Murray, Sir James G. Frazer, Joseph Campbell, and Carl Jung.

Thanks also to the Pagan Federation–Devon, Cornwall & Isles; the Gaia Gathering; the Canadian National Pagan Conference, Halifax, Canada; and The Summerland Spirit Circle in Clayton, Wisconsin, for granting me inner-sanctum interviews and sharing valuable information about culture and faith. I am grateful to the excellent metaphysical bookstores and shops: Avalon—All Things Rare and Magickal; Spiral Circle Bookstore, of Orlando, Florida; and the Occult Bookstore of Chicago for their collections and inspiration over the years.

I express my gratitude to Ms. Kathleen "epifania" Cavallo, a third-generation Strega, for her cooking assistance, and the countless chefs, cooks, and kitchen porters from countless pagan festivals and high holiday events that I have been privileged to attend, as well as the enchanted souls from numerous Renaissance fairs, re-enactment troupes, and historical events from all points across the United States, the United Kingdom, and Europe. I wish to recognize the Florida Historic Militia, Rupert's Bluecoats, Drake's Men, and The Men of Menendez of Saint Augustine, Florida, and also the Society for Creative Anachronisms for their contributions to the worlds of twelfth- to seventeeth-century living, and for affording me the grand opportunity to explore the often forgotten aspects of our rich and diverse histories. I thank you all for the good times and motivation you have given me.

This work is dedicated to the 80,000 or more souls who perished during The Burning Times in the name of man's arrogance and hate. I offer my gratitude and admiration for their steadfast spirit.

Bibliography

Ackerman, Roy. *The Chef's Apprentice Headline*. Great Britain, 1988.

Adamson, Melitta Weiss. *Daz Buuch Von Guuter Splse*. Krems, Austria: Medium Aevum Quotidianum Krems, 2000.

Adamson, Melitta Weiss. *Food in the Middle Ages*. New York: Garland Publishing, 1995.

Anderson, John L. (editor) *A Fifteenth Century Cookbook*. New York: Charles Scribner's Sons, 1962.

Aresty, Esther B. *The Exquisite Table: A History of French Cuisine*. Indianapolis, IN: Bobbs-Merrill, 1980.

Bayard, Tania, translator. *A Medieval Home Companion*. New York: Harper Collins, 1991.

Beebe, Ruth Anne. *Sallets, Humbles & Shrewsbery Cakes*. Boston: David R. Godine, 1976.

Best, Michael R. (editor). *The English Housewife*. Gervase Markham, Montreal: McGill-Queen's University Press, 1986.

Black, Maggie. *Food and Cooking in Medieval Britain*. London: English Heritage, 1985.

Booth, Sally Smith. *Hung, Strug & Potted: A History of Eating in Colonial America*. New York: Clarkson N. Potter, 1971.

Brears, Peter. *Food and Cooking in 17th Century Britain*. London: English Heritage, 1985.

Brears, Peter. *Food And Cooking in Sixteenth Century Britain*. London: English Heritage, 1985.

British Library, *Medieval and Earlier Manuscripts*. Retrieved (24 December, 2012) at http://britishlibrary.typepad.co.uk/digitisedmanuscripts/2012/04/unicorn-cookbook-found-at-the-british-library.html.

Bynum, Caroline Walker. *Holy Feast and Holy Fast: The Religious Significance of Food to Medieval Women*. Berkeley: University of California Press, 1987.

Caton, Mary Anne. *Fooles and Fricassees: Food in Shakespeare's England*. Seattle: University of Washington Press, 1999.

Chamberlain, E. R. *Everyday Life in Renaissance Times*. England: Jarrold and Sons Ltd., 1965.

Cosman Madeleine Pelner. *Medieval Holidays and Festivals*. New York: Charles Scribner's Sons, 1981.

Dapoundy, Andrew. *Dangerous Tastes*. Berkeley: University of California Press, 2000.

David, Elizabeth. *English Bread and Yeast Cookery*. New York: Penguin, 1979.

Davis, S. Williams. *Life in Elizabethan Days*. New York: Harper & Brothers, 1930.

Dawson, Imogen. *Food and Feasts in the Middle Ages*. New Discovery Books, 1994.

Dawson, Thomas. *The Good Housewife's Jewel*. East Sussex, England: Southover Press, 1996.

de la Falaise, Maxime. *Seven Centuries of English Cooking*. New York: Barnes and Noble Books, 1973.

Dover Publications. *Treasury of Medieval Illustrations*. Mineola, New York: Dover Ed edition, March 14, 2008.

Drummond & Wipoundraham. *The Englishman's Food*. J. Cape, 1957.

Gitlitz, David, and Linda Kay Davidson. *A Drizzle of Honey*. New York: St. Martin's Press, 1999.

Grewe, Rudolf, and Constance B. Hieatt. *Libbellus de Arte Coquinaria*. Tempe, AZ: Arizona Center for Medieval and Renaissance Studies, 2001.

Guy, Christian. *An Illustrated History of French Cuisine*. England: Bramhall House, 1962.

Hagen, Ann. *A Handbook of Anglo-Saxon Food: Processing and Consumption*. Nisslwawx, England: Anglo-Saxon Books,1992.

Hagen, Ann. *A Second Handbook of Anglo-Saxon Food & Drink: Production & Distribution.* Great Britain: Anglo-Saxon Books, 1995.

Hammond, P. A. *Food and Feast in Medieval England.* Gloucestershire, England: Alan Sutton, 1993.

Hartley, Dorothy. *Food in England.* Macdonald, 1954.

Hess, Karen. *Martha Washington's Booke of Cookery.* New York: Columbia University Press, 1995.

Hieatt, Constance, and Sharon Butler. *Curye on Inglysch.* England: Oxford University Press, 1985.

Hieatt, Constance B. *An Ordinance of Pottage.* London: Prospect Books, 1988.

Hieatt, Constance B., and Sharon Butler. *Pleyn Delit.* Toronto: University of Toronto Press, 1979.

Isitt, Verity. *Take a Buttock of Beefe.* England: Ashford Press, 1987.

Le Menagier de Paris, (Anonymous), ca. 1393.

Lysaght, Patricia. *Milk and Milk Products from Medieval to Modern Times.* Canongate Academic. Edinburgh, Scotland: Edinburgh University Press, 1994.

May, Robert. *The Accomplished Cook.* Devon, England: Prospect Books, 2000.

Mckendry, Maxime. *Seven Hundred Years of English Cooking.* Devon, England: Exeter Books, 1993.

Power, Eileen. *The Goodman of Paris "Le Menagier de Paris."* New York: Harcourt, Brace & Company, 1928.

Quennell, Marjorie, and C. H. B Quennell. *A History of Everyday Things in England.* New York: G. P. Putnam's Sons, date unknown.

Scully, Terence. *The Art of Cookery in the Middle Ages.* Suffolk, England: Boydell Press, 1995.

Society for Creative Anachronism, and the Arts and Sciences of the Middle Ages and Renaissance: http://www.pbm.com/~lindahl/arts_and_sciences.html.

Tannahill, Reay. *Food in History. New York:* New York: Stein and Day, 1973.

Wilson, C. Anne. *Banqueting Stuff.* Edinburgh, Scotland: Edinburgh University Press, 1990.

Wilson, C. Anne. *The Appetite and the Eye.* Edinburgh, Scotland: Edinburgh University Press, 1991.

Wilson, C. Anne. *Food and Drink in Britain: From the Stone Age to Recent Times.* New York: Penguin, 1984.

Young, Carolin C. *Apples of Gold in Settings of Silver.* New York: Simon & Schuster, 2002.

Greg Jenkins, PhD, MSc

𝕲𝖗𝖊𝖌 𝕵𝖊𝖓𝖐𝖎𝖓𝖘, PhD, (ThD) MSc, is a mental health professional, pastoral counselor, artist, and lecturer. He is the founder and co-director of Soulful Expressions: Independent Art Survey and Psychological Consulting, an organization that conducts research into the meaning of patient artwork. He is an avid folklorist and collector of urban legends and the many aspects of history that make up the diverse peoples in our world today. Greg is the author of *The Theban Oracle: Discover the Magic of the Ancient Alphabet That Changes Lives, Florida's Ghostly Legends and Haunted Folklore,* volumes 1–3, *Chronicles of the Strange and Uncanny in Florida,* and *Haunted Inns, Pubs & Eateries of St. Augustine.*